Reviews of
From Enemies to Partners:
Vietnam, the U.S. and Agent Orange

"There are no two people more qualified to speak on this subject than Charles Bailey and Dr. Le Ke Son. Their work has changed lives for the better. It has taken patience, perseverance and cooperation. We can all learn from their example."

—Christine Todd Whitman
Former governor of New Jersey and administrator
of the U.S. Environmental Protection Agency

"The impact and tragedy of war do not end with the silencing of guns. Agent Orange/dioxin's pernicious effect on the environment and on humans in Vietnam persists to this day, more than forty years after the official end of the war. Citizens of conscience in both the U.S. and Vietnam joined in the U.S.-Vietnam Dialogue Group on Agent Orange/Dioxin to address this legacy and to truly put the war behind us. It is the right thing to do for Vietnam, for the Vietnamese Agent Orange/dioxin victims, and for a full-fledged and mature relationship between our two countries. This compelling story needs to be told and who could better tell it than two of the chief architects of the work so far, Dr. Charles Bailey and Dr. Le Ke Son."

—Ambassador Ton Nu Thi Ninh
Former vice chair, Foreign Affairs Committee,
National Assembly of Vietnam

"Cleanup is something humans try to skirt, especially when a deadly toxin like Agent Orange caused such devastating damage. Drs. Charles Bailey and Le Ke Son took on the task of making policy makers deal with the task. This is a powerful book about all the problems they encountered focusing governments on the task and all that is left to do. Both sides in a war have soldiers they label 'heroes,' but Charles and Le Son are indefatigable heroes also."

—Pat Schroeder
Former member of Congress from Colorado

"*From Enemies to Partners* is a brilliant, unvarnished exploration of the use of Agent Orange during the Vietnam War. Charles Bailey and Dr. Le Ke Son paint a detailed, devastating portrait of the toxin's origins, its effects on Vietnam's ecosystem, and the relationship Vietnam and the U.S. must build to support communities still coping with the consequences of exposure. It's a must-read for anyone interested in understanding Agent Orange's complicated legacy and the way these two nations continue to navigate it."

—Darren Walker,
President, Ford Foundation

"This is exactly the book that is needed to advance the conversations surrounding Agent Orange, dioxin and the legacies of the American War in Vietnam. After decades of controversy, misinformation and distrust on all sides of this complex story, *From Enemies to Partners* offers a way forward that acknowledges the past while looking to the future. Bailey and Son move beyond the rhetoric and sensationalism that too often accompany this subject to provide thoughtful, rational and informed guidance on a range of important topics. This book should be read by leaders, policy makers and all students of wars and their legacies."

—Dr. Edwin A. Martini
Author of *Agent Orange: History, Science, and the Politics of Uncertainty*

From Enemies to Partners

VIETNAM, THE U.S. AND AGENT ORANGE

Le Ke Son
and
Charles R. Bailey

G. ANTON
Publisher

FROM ENEMIES TO PARTNERS
Copyright © 2017 by Le Ke Son and Charles R. Bailey

For permissions, contact the publisher:
Vivian Craig, General Manager
G. Anton Publishing, LLC
40 E. Chicago Avenue, Suite 129
Chicago, IL 60611
(vcraig@gantonpublishing.com)

This book was produced under a project of the American Council of Learned Societies, Center for Educational Exchange with Vietnam, 633 Third Avenue, New York, NY 10017.

Cover design: Niezeka
Cover images: (photo front/top) Spray planes, Vietnam 1968 (*Fiverr*); (photo front/bottom) American Ambassador to Vietnam David B. Shear and Vietnamese officials open the joint project to clean up dioxin at the Da Nang Airport, 2012 (*Charles R. Bailey*); (photo rear) Le Minh Chau of *Chau, Beyond the Lines*, in his studio in Ho Chi Minh City, 2014 (*Courtney Marsh*).

Excerpt from unpublished memoirs of Vo Quy printed with permission from the author.

Library of Congress Cataloging-in-Publication Data:

Names: Le, Son Ke | Bailey, Charles R.
Title: From Enemies to Partners: Vietnam, the U.S. and Agent Orange / Le Ke Son and Charles R. Bailey.
Description: Chicago, Illinois: G. Anton Publishing, LLC, 2017. Includes bibliographical references. |
Identifiers: ISBN 978-0-9993413-1-5 (hardcover) |
    ISBN 978-0-9993413-0-8 (paperback) |
    ISBN 978-0-9993413-2-2 (ebook)
Subjects: LCSH Vietnam War, 1961–1975—United States |
    Vietnam—History—1945–1975 | United States—History—1945 |
    United States—Foreign Relations—Vietnam | Vietnam—Foreign
    Relations—United States | Agent Orange—Health Aspects |
    Agent Orange—Environmental Aspects—Vietnam | Vietnam War,
    1961–1975—Chemical Warfare | BISAC POLITICAL SCIENCE /
    World / Asian |POLITICAL SCIENCE / International Relations / General
Classification: LCC E183.8.V5 .L4 2017 | DDC 327.73—dc23

To arrange a speaking engagement, contact Charles.BaileyADV@gmail.com.

G. ANTON
Publisher

This book is dedicated to

Professor Vo Quy
1929–2017

Ornithologist

Pioneer Advocate on Agent Orange

Founder of the Environmental Movement in Vietnam

Scientist

Teacher

Friend

Contents

About the Authors

"This weather's definitely not Vermont!" Senator Patrick Leahy observed with a smile as he arrived at the airport in steamy Da Nang. He was there to launch treatment of the first batch of dioxin-contaminated soils — the residue of Agent Orange used in the Vietnam War. In his prepared remarks to the officials, technicians and leaders of nongovernmental organizations assembled at the project site, he noted one goal: "to show that, after so many years, the U.S. did not ignore this problem. We returned and we are taking care of it." He also confirmed another goal: "to improve services for people with disabilities, regardless of the cause, including [those] which may have been caused by Agent Orange." This was a breakthrough statement after decades of dispute between the United States and Vietnam over Agent Orange. Later the same day, Senator Leahy became the first American elected official to visit a family with Agent Orange victims. It was April 19, 2014, and the senator's words and actions have moved U.S. and Vietnamese cooperation on Agent Orange to a new level.

Attending Senator Leahy that day were two people who had worked for years to arrive at this moment: Dr. Le Ke Son and Dr. Charles R. Bailey.

Son, a medical doctor with a PhD in toxicology, led the government of Vietnam's efforts to find an equitable way forward with the U.S. government. He was the former director of the Agent Orange Victims Fund at the Vietnam Red Cross and then concurrently director of the Office of the National Steering Committee for Overcoming Consequences of Toxic Chemicals Used by the U.S. in the War in Vietnam (known as Committee 33), vice director general of the Vietnam Environmental Administration and Vietnamese co-chair of the United States-Vietnam Joint Advisory Committee.

Bailey, a public policy specialist with a PhD in agricultural economics, was the Ford Foundation representative in Vietnam and headed the foundation's Hanoi office for a decade, from 1997 to 2007. He then led the Ford Foundation's initiative on Agent Orange/dioxin from New York before moving the project to the Aspen Institute in 2011. Bailey has worked to mobilize attention and resources in the United States, assess progress on the ground in Vietnam and present independent findings and analysis through public reports, meetings with officials and convenings of key stakeholders.

Bailey and Son's paths first crossed in December 2006, when the Ministry of Foreign Affairs recommended that the Ford Foundation work with the Office of Committee 33. The two have collaborated over the ensuing years to push for a breakthrough on Agent Orange, a campaign that would ensure that Vietnam and the United States cooperate to address the problems left by American use of Agent Orange during the Vietnam War. Son and Bailey retired in June 2014 and decided to again join forces — this time to write the story of how the United States and Vietnam finally began to resolve one of the twentieth century's iconic environmental and human disasters.

In writing this book they have drawn on their experiences, notes and documents accumulated over the last decade and a half as well as interviews with thirty-seven Americans and Vietnamese for their insights on what has happened and the way ahead. Son's knowledge, credibility and access now enable him to conduct a thorough review of Agent Orange/dioxin issues in Vietnam. Bailey's long engagement with Agent Orange/dioxin and his familiarity with the key players on the U.S. side enable him to explore the U.S. perspective fully.

From Enemies
to Partners

Patrick J. Leahy
United States Senator

"It would be hard to overstate the importance the Vietnamese give to addressing the needs of people who have been harmed. The legacy of Agent Orange, for years an issue that divided us, is now one that is bringing us together."

"I felt that instead of turning our backs on the problem we had a moral obligation to do something about it.

"My goal, to put it simply, was to turn Agent Orange from being a symbol of antagonism and resentment into another example of the U.S. and Vietnamese governments working together to address one of the most difficult and emotional legacies of the war.

"We have come a long way. We have further to go. . . .

"The funds should prioritize individuals who suffer from "severe mobility impairment and/or cognitive or developmental disabilities." We have limited funds, and we want them to be used to help those who are the most severely disabled.

—Congressional Record, 2010, and Center for Strategic and International Studies, 2015

Vu Khoan
Former Deputy Prime Minister of Vietnam

"The achievements in the current U.S.-Vietnam relationship are things that in previous years we could not have imagined. . . .

"We have a folklore story about crossing a bridge with a stone lying on it. There would be ways to do it: stepping over the stone to get to the other side, which is what we did, but the stone is still lying there, and people [are still] crossing back and forth with difficulty. So we have to find ways to solve it: either to move the stone aside or throw it into the river.

"I think U.S. politicians are smart enough to find a solution. I have no proposal but it [Agent Orange] is always an obstacle in our psychology. There were big stones on the bridge, which have already been removed, now there is only one small stone and we should find a way to solve this. . . .

"How do we know when we've gotten to the end? . . . It's not possible to give an answer to when it could be ended, but we should ask how we should end it. If you think towards how to end it, you'll find a solution.

—Hanoi, 2015

The Aftermath of War

The Vietnam War lasted twenty years, from November 1955 to April 1975.[1] A product of the Cold War, the Vietnam War was officially fought between North Vietnam and South Vietnam. The Soviet Union and China and their allies supported the armed forces of North Vietnam, while the United States, together with South Korea, Australia, Thailand and other allies, supported the armed forces of South Vietnam. Most of the fighting took place in the South, although the United States heavily bombed the North as well as parts of Laos and Cambodia. In the end, some 3.3 million Vietnamese soldiers and civilians on both sides were killed as well as 58,220 Americans. During the war, the United States deployed several military technologies, including napalm, helicopter gunships and herbicides sprayed from the air.

No one today can disagree with these facts: In 1961, the United States military, in its attempts to assist the government controlling what was known then as South Vietnam, began spraying the herbicide Agent Orange and other herbicides in Vietnam to defoliate forests and destroy food crops in order to deny cover and sustenance to opposition forces. The Agent Orange and some of the other herbicides were contaminated with dioxin, a toxic substance. Between 1961 and 1970, at several air bases in South Vietnam, 19.5 million gallons of the herbicides were stored, mixed, handled and loaded into aircraft for the spraying campaign. The spraying denuded forests and destroyed crops across 10,160 square miles of the country. That 10,160 square miles compares to South Vietnam's entire size of 67,108 square miles, so the denuded area represents 15 percent of the entire country. Some other comparisons suggest the extent of the sprayed areas: the American state of Massachusetts has a total of 10,555 square miles, and Belgium has 11,787 square miles. And besides Vietnam, areas of Cambodia and Laos along the border with Vietnam were also sprayed with herbicides by the United States. That is only the land picture. As many as 4.1 million Vietnamese and 2.8 million American military personnel may have been exposed to the herbicide. Finally, in 1970, the Nixon Administration ordered a halt to the spraying program.

Since 1991, scientists at the United States Institute of Medicine have shown dioxin to be a risk factor in a growing number of illnesses and birth defects, and their research is corroborated by the work of Vietnamese scientists.[2] In 2007, thirty-two years after the end of the war, the governments of Vietnam and the United States began to address this war legacy on the ground in Vietnam.

To fully understand the legacy of Agent Orange in Vietnam, one needs to understand the past — how we got here. This book is a lot about the past actually, but the book's aim is to call for and guide future action. There are a large number of victims of Agent Orange in Vietnam — nobody knows the exact number for sure. Most of them live at home with profound disabilities linked to exposure to dioxin. Although Vietnam has done much to help them, they and their caregivers still await a threshold level of assistance so that they can lead lives of greater dignity and comfort. Dioxin contamination at the Bien Hoa Air Base needs to be cleaned up to stop further exposure of the tens of thousands of people living nearby. The cleanup is a massive undertaking that will cost several hundred million dollars and take a decade. Most of this book, therefore, has a practical focus. It presents authoritative answers to key questions that will provide the basis for future progress.

How and why the U.S. military used Agent Orange and other military herbicides fifty years ago is a complex story. The aftermath and consequences of its use are even more complex, keenly felt and still hotly debated. Until quite recently, the investigations and scientific studies carried out by the government of Vietnam since 1980 were classified and therefore unavailable to journalists, scientists, other governments and concerned members of the public, both in Vietnam and elsewhere. Good science, with global heft and credibility, requires scientists with advanced training who work in modern facilities and publish in international peer-reviewed journals. While there are many fine scientists in Vietnam, the scientific infrastructure has only begun to catch up with them in the last decade. Vietnamese scientists made their first presentations to an international meeting of peer scientists on dioxin, the environment and health in 2006.[3] In 2009 the Ministry of Natural Resources and Environment opened Vietnam's first laboratory capable of testing at the level of parts per quadrillion for dioxin in soils, sediments, foodstuffs and human blood and breast milk.[4]

The Language of Agent Orange/Dioxin

The militaries of the United States and the Saigon government described the chemicals they used in their spraying programs as herbicides and their intended purpose as defoliants to clear forest cover and destroy crops. The most frequently used herbicide was a mixture of 2-4 D and 2,4,5-T, barrels of which were coded with an orange stripe on the side, which led to the popular name Agent Orange.

The careless manufacture by the United States of Agent Orange (as well as some of the other herbicides that were used) created an unintended but extremely toxic contaminant — dioxin. Many authors commonly label the impact of the herbicides on the environment and human health in Vietnam as the result of Agent Orange, whereas Agent Orange was just the carrier for the actual toxic contaminant, dioxin. More recently, writers and others use the label "Agent Orange/dioxin" to capture both the origin and the consequence of the spraying program. Writers in the Vietnamese language render "Agent Orange" as "toxic chemical" or, wrongly, "orange-colored poison." Some of the legal documents of the government of Vietnam and some newspaper articles in Vietnam and elsewhere use the phrase "toxic chemical" instead of "herbicides" or "Agent Orange," which leads to one more phrase, "chemical warfare." High-level committees established by the government of Vietnam to address Agent Orange/dioxin have names like the National Committee for Investigating the Consequences of Toxic Chemicals Used by the U.S. in the War in Vietnam (Committee 10-80) or the National Steering Committee for Overcoming Consequences of Toxic Chemicals Used by the U.S. in the War in Vietnam (Committee 33).

The acronym VAVA stands for the Vietnam Association of Victims of Agent Orange/Dioxin, an organization advocating on behalf of victims of Agent Orange/dioxin. These terms are rooted in Vietnamese government positions related to scientific definitions and the international conventions on chemical weapons.

These different wordings and labels have led to different conclusions and ways to handle the consequences of the herbicides. For their part, the United States Department of State and the United States Agency for International Development (USAID) do not use the term "Agent Orange victim." The U.S. Congress, however, does use it.[5] In this book we employ this term, which is commonly used in Vietnam to designate those people with disabilities whose condition is likely to be associated with dioxin exposure. After numerous scientific discussions, the phrase "Agent Orange/dioxin" or "Agent Orange" has become the most compelling, so it is used more often than other phrases and, in fact, it has been accepted in the scientific discussions and official bilateral exchanges between Vietnam and the United States.

This book is about the particular struggle to address the effects of Agent Orange's use during the Vietnam War. It also tells how it is possible to address a serious and complex problem in the face of profound political and legal resistance. We have written this book for policy decision makers, advocates and donors, journalists, program managers who work on disability assistance and clean up, and students of war and its legacies.

Each chapter opens with a paragraph summarizing its contents. Readers seeking specific content may review these summaries to determine whether they wish to read the full chapter.

How We Got Here and What's Next

How We Got Here

B etween 1975, when the Vietnam War ended, and 2006, Agent Orange was an extremely sensitive and controversial subject. Official views were polarized, information was scant, disagreement was rife and suspicions on both sides ran high. In consequence, there were few resources to address the issue, and nongovernmental organizations (NGOs) and other donors kept well clear of the subject. Despite the silence and the inaction, the government of Vietnam budgeted increasing amounts annually for income supplements and other supports for Agent Orange victims and their families and substantial sums for containment and cleanup of dioxin contamination at former U.S. military bases. However, in this period foreign assistance was negligible for programs to address this toxic legacy of the Vietnam War.

Events in 2006 proved a turning point: new attention was brought to Agent Orange by the American press in advance of U.S. President George W. Bush's visit to Vietnam for the meeting of members of APEC (Asia-Pacific Economic Cooperation); Bush's joint statement with Vietnam's President Nguyen Minh Triet, which included a reference to this

war legacy;[1] open sharing of information by the Vietnamese government; swift follow-up by the U.S. Embassy and the Ford Foundation in
Hanoi and a decision by the American Congress for an initial appropriation. These events led to an inflow of foreign public and private
funding for cleanup and assistance to Agent Orange victims. Since
2007, key Vietnamese and American officials and nongovernment players in both countries have helped move the issue of Agent Orange in
Vietnam to a subject of active cooperation between the governments
of Vietnam and the United States. This process has attracted a wider
range of participants, created new plans and growing appropriations,
and led to greater clarity and specificity. For example, thanks to the U.S.
Congress, American assistance for health and disability, despite being
delivered "regardless of cause," now targets people living in the heavily
sprayed provinces in southern Vietnam (2013)[2] and within those areas
the severely disabled (2015).[3] In sum, the two countries have evolved a
shared sense of responsibility for a humanitarian response. As of 2016,
the U.S. State Department described the American position on Agent
Orange/dioxin as follows:

> U.S. assistance also seeks to support Vietnam's response to climate
> change and other environmental challenges, including remediating
> Agent Orange/dioxin contamination, strengthening the country's
> health and education systems, *and assisting vulnerable populations.*
> The United States and Vietnam successfully concluded the first
> phase of dioxin remediation at Da Nang International Airport and
> has committed to partnering with Vietnam to make a significant
> contribution to the cleanup of dioxin contamination at Bien Hoa
> Air Base.[4]

As of 2018, the United States Congress has appropriated $231.2 mil-
lion, split between assistance for people with disabilities and dioxin
cleanup, and the U.S. government is now the single largest foreign con-
tributor to this effort. The funds and follow-up that provoked and lev-
eraged the American government response after all these years came
in large part from the Ford Foundation, which provided $17.1 million
between 2000 and 2011.

The U.S. commitment to clean up the dioxin it left behind in Da
Nang and Bien Hoa is historic. Japan may be the only other example of

comparable scale in which a country has voluntarily paid to clean up the environmental damage caused by its military. In 1999, Japan agreed to locate and destroy some 700,000 chemical weapons that the Imperial Army buried across northeastern China at the end of World War II. This work is continuing and may ultimately cost $1.6 billion.[5] The U.S. commitment to Vietnam overturns earlier concerns for creating a precedent for claims from other countries impacted by the actions of U.S. armed forces. The State Department Fact Sheet also notes that the United States will support Vietnam by "assisting vulnerable populations." Vietnamese with disabilities are among the vulnerable population, and thus the United States' support for health and disability services in Vietnam includes Vietnam's Agent Orange victims. Indeed, as the U.S. government's work on Agent Orange has grown, so has it accepted responsibility in practice, not expressly but by its actions. And statements by U.S. government officials — Senator Patrick Leahy and successive secretaries of state — have acknowledged as much.

What's Next

The United States' turn toward involvement with Agent Orange/dioxin cleanup and disability assistance is a story of political evolution from a taboo topic to a subject of humanitarian engagement. It is an instructive example of the evolution of moral sensitivity.

George Washington, America's first president, said in his Farewell Address, "Virtue or morality is a necessary spring of popular government." Americans believe their government acts on their behalf and that those actions should be based on principles of morality. In our view, the three pillars of morality are curiosity (a positive desire to know and to understand), empathy (attention to others' feelings) and reciprocity (if others follow the same rule, you'll be treated well). Three principles follow from this: Americans learn at an early age that if you've made a mess you should clean it up. If you've harmed someone you should help them and make it right insofar as possible. And some things can't wait; they require urgent attention. All three principles apply to the Agent Orange legacy in Vietnam.

Countries don't think about the aftermath when they go to war, although we know that wars cast shadows into the future that last long after the guns have fallen silent and the soldiers have left the field of battle. Countries are reluctant to address the consequences of their military actions on other countries' land due to cost and precedent — environmental remediation and health and disability assistance for victims are astonishingly expensive, and no country wants to create a precedent compelling it to clean up the messes it has made elsewhere. International law to limit the impact of war on human health and the environment offers no solution because it is weak and lacks enforcement mechanisms. Even the treaties and conventions signed after the end of the Vietnam War make broad exceptions for military activity.[6]

The United States considers itself to have no legal obligation to Vietnam under the terms of a normalization agreement reached in 1995, and attempts by Vietnamese plaintiffs to win damages in American courts have failed. The United States continues to assert that there is insufficient evidence to show that the Agent Orange that it brought to and sprayed in Vietnam caused the diseases and birth defects the Vietnamese people suffer. For its part, it is difficult for Vietnam to prove causation in individual cases. Even if Vietnam could definitively determine who was affected by Agent Orange, however, the United States could still worry about actually admitting responsibility.

We think the signals around Agent Orange/dioxin are positive now but far too weak. We fear that without a bolder and more broad-based commitment by the U.S. government, official American assistance will dwindle in a few years for health and disability services in Vietnam. The Agent Orange issue has come a long way in Washington and there is now an emerging sense that Americans do have a moral obligation to stay the course with Vietnam on Agent Orange, but more champions and greater public awareness are needed.

Walter Isaacson, renowned biographer and former president of the Aspen Institute, emphasizes this point: "The U.S. was responsible for leaving dioxins and other problems in Vietnam. . . . I think that Agent Orange is a moral issue, and it goes to our decency as Americans and our willingness to take responsibility for what we did. . . . In our political system today it's very hard to fund anything. Americans make the mistake of not paying attention to a problem for a long period of time. They move on to other issues. So for most Americans this is not an issue they would ever think about on a given day, whereas for people in Vietnam it's a more present issue. So in America one challenge is that we need to continue to raise awareness of this issue both in the government and among the people."[7]

Ambassador Ton Nu Thi Ninh, a former member of Vietnam's National Assembly, observes, "The time for Agent Orange arrived when the relationship matured and it was easier for the Vietnamese to hear about human rights without becoming defensive and for the U.S. side [to understand that] mentioning Agent Orange was not going to destroy the relationship. . . . [This issue] has moved some but it has a way to go. Just make sure that the American government doesn't push it off to the side of the road, but the same [is true] for our officials. They tend to want to make it easier to talk about trade and economic cooperation. I think that the expectations will come from [our] society, the pressure . . . the public will keep on them."[8]

In this case, U.S. moral concerns coincide with American strategic ones. The majority of Vietnamese people do not recriminate against Americans for their actions during a now long-ago war; indeed, Vietnam has become one of the most pro-American countries in Asia.[9] Relations between Vietnam and the United States have now reached a historic high following the signing of the U.S.-Vietnam Comprehensive Partnership in 2013 and the celebration of twenty years of diplomatic relations in 2015. Trade between the two countries has nearly tripled in the last seven years; it now exceeds $45 billion annually and will continue to grow. Close to 19,000 Vietnamese now study in the United States each year. The two countries cooperate on maritime security in the South China Sea, and U.S. Navy ships have begun making calls at Cam Ranh Bay, a deep-water harbor in central Vietnam.[10] Freedom of navigation has been a U.S. foreign policy goal since the American Revolution of 1776 and nowhere today is this goal more overtly challenged than in the South China Sea. Vietnam is the strongest partner for the United States in the region as it addresses this challenge.

The majority of Vietnamese who left the country in 1975 and later settled in the United States and became citizens. They and their children and grandchildren now number some two million Americans, but many of them contribute to businesses and charitable causes in Vietnam and maintain family ties. Vietnamese Americans have a special opportunity and indeed a mandate to lead America out of the lingering legacy of Agent Orange. Vietnamese Americans' insight into Vietnam and what it means to help gives them a powerful credibility in saying to other Americans: Agent Orange — let's fix this; it's a humanitarian concern we can do something about. Indeed, America will only finally turn the corner on Agent Orange when Vietnamese Americans speak up and say to U.S. political leaders: Vietnam — it's an important country. Let's fix this now. It's the morally right thing to do.

Building on the two countries' substantial accomplishments to date, we call on the United States and Vietnam to complete a joint humanitarian effort to resolve the legacy of Agent Orange/dioxin.

Vietnam and the United States could end the legacy of Agent Orange. It would require agreement by leaders at the highest level of each government. Vietnam would need to say to the United States that resolving this legacy is now among their highest priorities in the bilateral relationship and state their expectations. The United States would need to consider the size and scope of the assistance to provide over a number of years.

In the absence of such a settlement, the present system of American annual appropriations needs to continue.

In this case, the two governments should create a joint multiyear plan or framework agreement for bilateral cooperation and a joint commission to oversee its implementation. The joint commission would meet twice a year with official and non-official members from each country. Former Deputy Prime Minister Vu Khoan has urged that future deliberations focus on what should be done to close the Agent Orange legacy rather than when it will be closed. The two governments already agree the next step for cleanup is to remediate the Bien Hoa Air Base. The multiyear plan can incorporate these actions. It should also establish a common understanding and agreement on the criteria and standards for allocating American in-kind services to children and young adults with disabilities and their families and to building capacities for continuing services to these groups once the foreign assistance has ended. It would also spell out priorities for possible assistance for reproductive health services, newborn screening and infant healthcare. The plan would provide a framework for the contributions of other donors and become the basis for closer cooperation with the government of Vietnam and Vietnamese nongovernmental organizations.

In addition, the two governments should fund and launch a multi-year program of scientific research on the long-term impacts of dioxin on human health and well-being. Vietnam is already a leader in epidemiological, genetic and environmental studies of dioxin, and its presentations of findings have attracted worldwide scientific attention at the annual International Symposium on Halogenated Persistent Organic Pollutants. However, research capacity is still limited in relation to the need for better scientific understanding of the nature and impact of dioxin and other environmental pollutants.

There are several positive steps that each government can take on its own that will ensure the effectiveness of their joint efforts.

For the United States:

- Since 2007, the U.S. Congress has appropriated increasing amounts for disabilities assistance and dioxin remediation in Vietnam. To maximize the permanent impact of this U.S. assistance to Vietnam, the president's annual budgets for USAID and the Department of Defense should include the funding necessary to continue these important programs.

- Disabilities assistance should focus on the most heavily sprayed provinces and the most severely disabled people living in those places.

- U.S. disability assistance programs should aim for permanent improvements both in the lives of Vietnamese with disabilities and in the capacities of local government to provide services to them.

- The State Department and USAID should seek out and actively encourage other bilateral donors as well as American and other foreign corporations in Vietnam to support health and disability projects through their development assistance and corporate philanthropy programs.

For Vietnam:

- The government, in particular the Ministry of Defense and the Bien Hoa Peoples Committee, should immediately collect and destroy fish and other aquatic animals in all lakes on the Bien Hoa Air Base and all dioxin-contaminated lakes outside the air base and prevent their reintroduction.

- The government should issue one decree that applies to all Agent Orange victims equally and provides benefits that are consistent, comprehensive and long term.

- The decree should define Agent Orange victims as people with diseases and disabilities related to dioxin and who live or have lived in sprayed or dioxin-contaminated areas. This provision is approximate and humanitarian, but it is still the best approach in light of current scientific understanding and practical realities. It is also the approach the U.S. government uses toward its veterans.

- The government should review the structure, responsibilities and authority of collaborating agencies to ensure effectiveness. Specific tasks assigned to ministries, sectors and relevant agencies should be incorporated in one decree on the remedy for Agent Orange impacts on Vietnam.

- The government should consolidate existing information on people with disabilities, their situations and their needs, for every district and province, beginning with the heavily sprayed provinces. Then it could be made available to donors to inform decisions on programs and the overall levels of required resources.

- The government should publish an annual report of expenditures on dioxin remediation, social services and allowances for people with disabilities, including those impacted by dioxin, and related costs. Such information would highlight the Vietnamese government's leading role in addressing these challenges and would help encourage a more generous response from U.S. policy makers.

- The government should bring the Agent Orange issue before the annual meeting of the official Vietnam Development Forum to call for donors' support for health and disabilities projects in their programs of development assistance.

Some actions are not helpful to progress and should be discontinued. These include characterizing Vietnamese as "Agent Orange victims" when their health status or disability does not meet the criteria laid down by the Ministry of Health. Disability has many causes, and only about 15 percent of Vietnamese with disabilities can trace their disability to indirect exposure to dioxin. Another is describing the Agent Orange legacy as huge, unmanageable and long lasting, which ignores or minimizes the progress the two governments have achieved together since 2007. While there will never be a complete resolution of the diverse impacts of dioxin exposure, it is possible to make substantial progress through sustainable programs of services to the severely disabled and cleanup of dioxin-contaminated soils.

Another candidate for discontinuation is further legal challenges in the courts. On the one hand, Vietnam has asked the U.S. government to help overcome the consequences of Agent Orange, but on the other, Vietnam has sued the U.S. chemical companies. These activities are contradictory and counterproductive. It is an oversimplified notion that they create pressure on the U.S. government to help Vietnam. It is more likely that they trigger adverse reactions from some U.S. government agencies. Lawsuits in the United States and other countries did lead to widespread international understanding that Agent Orange has a continuing legacy in Vietnam. However, they have not produced a solution to what is essentially a political and humanitarian issue.

CHAPTER ONE

Is There Still Dioxin Pollution in Southern Vietnam?

Vietnamese and foreign scientists have for many years tested soils and sediments for dioxin in the areas sprayed in the 1960s and at former U.S. military bases in southern Vietnam. While they have found dioxin, it exists today at levels below, and often substantially below, established thresholds for cleanup. Dioxin is present at levels requiring remediation in soils and sediments at the three former American bases at Bien Hoa, Da Nang and Phu Cat. At Bien Hoa and Da Nang, scientists have also found elevated dioxin levels in the blood of airport workers, fishermen and people consuming fish raised at the airport. Remediation of dioxin at Phu Cat is finished, and Da Nang will be finished in 2018. The Bien Hoa Air Base and the lakes surrounding it, however, remain heavily contaminated. Authorities need to stop the further use of those lakes for raising fish and ducks.

What is the fate of the dioxin that contaminated Agent Orange and other military herbicides used in southern Vietnam now over fifty years ago? Does it still threaten public health, and if so, what is being done about it? We examine the evidence and the outcomes for the heavily sprayed provinces themselves and for the former American military bases where the herbicides were stored and mixed and then loaded onto spray planes, and for the Vietnamese today who are living nearby. We then discuss other sources of dioxin contamination and how Vietnam is managing them.

Vietnamese scientists and their foreign partners have prioritized the heavily sprayed provinces as the most likely sites of residual dioxin from Agent Orange and related herbicides. Over seventeen years, from 1993 to 2010, in the numerous studies reported below as well as others, the scientists analyzed thousands of samples of soil and sediment and hundreds of samples of fish and other animals as well as human blood and breast milk.

In almost all cases measured, dioxin levels in sprayed areas were below, and often substantially below the government of Vietnam's established thresholds of 120 ppt TEQ (parts per trillion toxic equivalent) for residential soils in rural areas and 150 ppt TEQ for pond and lake sediments. (An explanation of these terms can be found in Appendix 1.)[1] In some instances, dioxin could not be detected at all. The only exceptions were several soil samples in one area of Sa Thay District in Kon Tum Province.[2] Dioxin residues from Agent Orange are not a direct threat to anyone living and working in or visiting virtually all areas of Vietnam today. Sunlight has long ago broken down any dioxin remaining in the surface of soils, and many years of rainfall have dissipated the remaining dioxin in soils, and sediments.

Scientists also prioritized former U.S. military bases, hypothesizing that dioxin-contaminated hot spots or point sources of contamination would be identified where the toxic chemicals were handled, stored and used continually over a long period of time.[3] Results show that of the many former military installations, only three have levels of dioxin contamination that exceed Vietnamese thresholds. These are the airports at Phu Cat, Da Nang and Bien Hoa, where contaminated soils and sediments have been contained (Phu Cat) or are in the process of being remediated (Da Nang and Bien Hoa). The high levels of dioxin in the blood and breast milk of people who worked on the airport in Da Nang and people who are consuming fish, ducks, snails and other aquatic animals produced on the Bien Hoa Air Base remain a matter of great concern.

Persistent organic pollutants (POPs), of which dioxin is one, have many potential sources in the industrializing economy of modern

Vietnam. The Vietnam Environmental Administration has developed technical capacities and introduced regulatory standards for detecting and cleaning up pollutants in the future.

Dioxin Threshold Levels

Many countries have established threshold levels for dioxin in soils by type of use and for sediment in water bodies. Dioxin in excess of these thresholds triggers assessment and remediation. The table shows these threshold trigger levels for Vietnam,[4] Japan and the United States.[5]

Table 1.1. Dioxin Threshold Levels

Soils & Sediment	Vietnam	Japan	United States
Annual cropland soils	40 ppt TEQ	N/A	N/A
Forests & perennial treeland soils	100 ppt TEQ	N/A	N/A
Rural residential use soils	120 ppt TEQ	N/A	50 ppt TEQ
Stream & pond sediments	150 ppt TEQ	150 ppt TEQ	N/A
Urban residential use soils	300 ppt TEQ	N/A	51 ppt TEQ
Recreational use soils	600 ppt TEQ	N/A	N/A
Commercial/ industrial use soils	1,200 ppt TEQ	1,000 ppt TEQ	730 ppt TEQ

Note: ppt: parts per trillion/TEQ: Toxicity equivalent

Soils that are used for production of food and timber, or with which people have frequent contact, have the lowest thresholds. Stream and pond sediments are soils found in freshwater at the bottom of streams and ponds and in marine environments. Sediments have the potential to release dioxin into the food chain and dioxins tend to bio-accumulate up the food chain and can be found in the tissues of humans.[6] Commercial and industrial use soils include soils at airports and air bases. Government of Vietnam regulations require remediation of areas that exceed the above limits. In addition, commercial use soils containing dioxin in the range of 500 to 1,200 ppt TEQ and sediments in the range of 50 to 150 ppt TEQ require continuing monitoring. The Vietnam threshold levels are similar to other international standards and are therefore the standard by which to judge the significance of dioxin residues remaining from the spraying of Agent Orange.

Sprayed Areas in the South

Vietnamese scientists have collaborated with scientists from Canada, Japan, Germany, the Czech Republic, New Zealand and the United States since the 1990s to investigate and assess the levels of residual dioxin in Vietnam. They prioritized the areas that had been heavily sprayed based on herbicide spray maps and data from the United States Department of Defense. Analyses by Westing (1976),[7] Schecter (1995)[8] and Stellman (2003)[9] contributed significantly to understanding what became of the dioxin in Agent Orange.

From 1961 through 1970, U.S. forces used an estimated 73,780,253 liters (or about 19.5 million gallons) of herbicides[10] to defoliate coastal mangroves, clear inland forests and vegetation around roads, railroads, power lines, canals and military bases, and to destroy crops. These tactics were intended to deprive opposition forces of natural cover and to reduce the food supplies available to them. Nearly all the herbicides were sprayed from C-123 aircraft. About 2 percent was used to clear vegetation around military bases with backpack sprayers, trucks and helicopters.

Table 1.2. Stellman: Liters and percent distribution of herbicides sprayed in the Republic of South Vietnam, 1962-1971, by agent[*] and year of spraying.[**]

Year	Purple	Pink	Orange	White	Blue	Unstated	Total	Cumulative Percentage
1962	142,085				10,031		152,117	0.2%
1963	340,433						340,433	0.7%
1964	831,162				15,619		846,781	1.8%
1965	579,092	50,312	1,868,194			18,927	2,516,525	5.2%
1966			7,602,390	2,179,450	59,809	126,474	9,968,124	18.7%
1967			12,528,833	5,141,117	1,518,029	86,288	19,274,267	44.9%
1968			8,747,064	8,353,143	1,289,144	249,750	18,639,101	70.1%
1969			12,679,579	3,987,100	1,035,385	274,291	17,976,356	94.5%
1970			2,251,876	845,464	762,665	96,509	3,956,514	99.9%
1971				50,251	50,698	9,085	110,034	100.0%
TOTALS	1,892,773	50,312	45,677,937	20,556,525	4,741,381	861,325	73,780,253	
Percent	2.6%	0.1%	61.9%	27.9%	6.4%	1.2%	100.0%	

* Data do not include 947 l Dinoxol and 548 l Trinoxol sprayed during tests in 1961.
** Data are taken from corrected HERBS file.

Two-thirds of the total volume of herbicides — 47,621,022 liters — were contaminated with dioxin. These were the herbicides color coded Agents Orange, Pink and Purple. Operation Ranch Hand, the U.S. military's code name for the spraying of herbicides in Southeast Asia, ultimately sprayed 1,679,734 hectares (or 4,150,713 acres) with these dioxin-contaminated herbicides, or about 15 percent of the area of Southern Vietnam. Over the nine years of the program, Ranch Hand sprayed many areas repeatedly.[11] According to Stellman, "Among the hamlets with some population data, 3,181 were sprayed directly and at least 2.1 million but perhaps as many as 4.8 million people would have been present during the spraying."[12]

Target areas for Ranch Hand and the intensity of spraying in gallons per square kilometer are shown on the map on page 112.

The most intensively sprayed provinces are the areas where one would most expect to find residual dioxin today. From north to south they are: Quang Tri (Cam Lo and Gio Linh), Thua Thien-Hue (Aluoi), Kon Tum (Sa Thay), Binh Duong (Tan Uyen), Binh Phuoc (Bu Gia Map), Tay Ninh (Tan Bien), Dong Nai (Ma Da), Ho Chi Minh City (Can Gio) and Ca Mau. Vietnamese scientists have also assessed the levels of dioxin residues in the Nha Trang Bay and the estuary of the Saigon River. All these areas were highly affected, and they provide a more or less complete picture of the situation today in areas where dioxin residues may potentially remain from the war.

Cam Lo and Gio Linh, Quang Tri Province[13]

Quang Tri Province lies along the border between the South and the North of Vietnam during the war. At the time it was called the Demilitarized Zone (DMZ), and the struggles there were the fiercest. A total of 2,852,843 liters of defoliants and herbicides, including 2,204,348 liters of Agent Orange, were sprayed over this area.

From 2000 to 2004, the Ministry of Health's Committee for Investigating the Consequences of the Chemicals Used by the U.S. in the War in Vietnam (the 10-80 Committee), and the Vietnam-Russia Tropical Center collected and measured dioxin concentrations in a total of ninety-seven samples, including seventy soil samples, fifteen sediment samples, two water samples and ten fish samples. The analyses examined the level of TCDD in the soil samples. TCDD (2,3,7,8-tetrachlorodibenzo-p-dioxin) is the most toxic of the dioxin compounds. The toxicity of other dioxins is measured in relation to TCDD. When 2,3,7,8-TCDD accounts for 80 to 100 percent of the toxicity equivalent (TEQ) in the sample, it is presumptive evidence that the dioxin in the sample came from Agent Orange or one of the other herbicides used in Operation Ranch Hand. The soil-sample levels of TCDD ranged from non-detectable levels to a maximum of 10.4 ppt TEQ; in the sediment samples dioxin ranged from non-detectable levels to a maximum of 3.4 ppt TEQ; no dioxin was found in the water samples. For the fish samples, the level of TCDD ranged from 0 to a maximum of 0.13 ppt.

Aluoi District, Thua Thien-Hue Province

Aluoi District is a valley lying along the border with Laos in the mountains west of the city of Hue. A reported 4,532,729 liters of defoliants and herbicides, including 3,445,604 liters of Agent Orange, were sprayed over this area.

From 1996 to 1999 the 10-80 Committee and Hatfield Consultants collected 101 soil samples, twenty sediment samples and nineteen fish samples and tested them for dioxin. The greatest concentration, 877 ppt TEQ, was in two soil samples from the former U.S. Army air base in the valley at A So (referred to as Ashau by the United States). Two other former air bases showed lower concentrations — the average sample concentration at Aluoi Air Base for nine samples was 12 ppt TEQ and the average for seven samples at Ta Bat Air Base was 13 ppt TEQ. Of the twenty sediment samples, the average concentration of TCDD was 5.6 ppt TEQ. The average concentration of TCDD in nineteen samples of grass carp fat analyzed was 16.1 ppt. The 10-80 Committee and Hatfield also collected and analyzed human blood and breast milk and found dioxin. They were thus able to show the chain of contamination from soils and sediments to fish to people.

Sa Thay, Kon Tum Province

Kon Tum Province is a mountainous area in central Vietnam east of the junction of the borders of Laos and Cambodia. On August 10, 1961,[14] the U.S. military first tested the use of herbicides with spraying flights along Highway 14, from Ngoc Hoi District across Sa Ly Hill and up to the northern area of Kon Tum Town, the provincial capital. In the ensuing decade, 3,921,047 liters of defoliants and herbicides, including 2,861,154 liters of Agent Orange, were sprayed on Kon Tum, mostly in Sa Thay and Ngoc Hoi Districts.

The Vietnam-Russia Tropical Center in 2003 analyzed fourteen samples of soil and six samples of sediments from Sa Nhon commune, in Sa Thay District, but did not detect dioxin in any of these samples.

Le Xuan Canh and colleagues of the Vietnam Academy of Science and Technology took fifteen samples of soil and sediments in three areas in 2010. These were a very heavily sprayed area, Sac Ly (Sa Thay District, Kon Tum Province), a less sprayed area, Cha Val, (Nam Giang District, Quang Nam Province) and, as a control, Chu Mon Ray (Kon Tum Province), where there was no spraying. TCDD concentrations in soil samples from the foot of the mountain ranges in Sac Ly ranged from 482 to 845 ppt TEQ, and the sediment samples ranged from 135 to 619 ppt TEQ. The concentration of TCDD in the sediment of Cha Val ranged from 107 to 430 ppt TEQ. Dioxin was measured at 345 ppt TEQ in soil samples from Chu Mon Ray, where there was no spraying.

These three areas of Kon Tum Province call for further investigation.

Tan Uyen and Phu Giao, Binh Duong Province

Binh Duong Province, an area of lower-lying hills, lies to the north of Ho Chi Minh City. The province was heavily sprayed during the war, receiving 5,476,469 liters of defoliants and herbicides, including 2,557,908 liters of Agent Orange.

In 2000, the Vietnam-Russia Tropical Center collected nineteen samples of soil in Binh My commune that showed an average dioxin concentration of only 14 ppt TEQ. Four soil samples in Chanh My commune showed a dioxin concentration level of 5.6 ppt TEQ. The fourteen samples of fish from these two communes contained dioxin levels of 3 to 4 ppt TEQ.

In another study, scientists at the Vietnam Institute for Tropical Technology and Environmental Protection collected thirty-six soil samples and four sediment samples in 2009 from Tan Uyen and Phu Giao Districts. The level of dioxin in the soil samples ranged from 1 to 27 ppt TEQ (4.8 ppt TEQ on average). In the four sediment samples, the dioxin concentration ranged from 1 to 5.3 ppt TEQ (2.5 ppt TEQ on average).

Bu Gia Map, Phuoc Long, Binh Phuoc Province

Some 9,420,722 liters of defoliants and herbicides, including 4,822,006 liters of Agent Orange, were sprayed over Binh Phuoc Province during the war. Bu Gia Map and Dong Phu Districts were sprayed the most heavily.

The Vietnam-Russia Tropical Center tested sixteen soil samples, six sediment samples and two fish samples in 2003 from Duc Hanh commune of Phuoc Long Town. The tests showed that the average dioxin concentration in the soil samples was about 1 ppt TEQ, the sediment samples approximately 1 ppt TEQ, and the fish samples less than 0.1 ppt TEQ.

In 2010, Pham Van Thanh and colleagues of the Vietnam Institute for Geosciences and Mineral Resources (Ministry of Natural Resources and Environment) tested 153 soil samples from agricultural lands and forests in Bu Gia Map, finding TCDD levels from 0.4 to 8.6 ppt.

Tan Bien, Dau Tieng, Tay Ninh Province

Tay Ninh was an especially heavily sprayed province: 5,238,098 liters of defoliant chemicals, including 2,210,483 liters of Agent Orange, were sprayed over Tay Ninh, mostly in Tan Bien and Tan Chau Districts. Dau Tieng Lake lies in Dau Tieng District of Tay Ninh and Hon Quan District of neighboring Binh Phuoc Province. The lake has a surface area of 45.6 square kilometers and a volume of about 1.58 billion cubic meters and plays a very important role in providing water for household and irrigation activities in Tay Ninh and Binh Phuoc.

Matsuda (Japan) et al. (1993) tested fifty-four soil samples from areas around Dau Tieng Lake and found TCDD only in fourteen samples, ranging from 1.2 to 38.4 ppt TEQ (an average of 14 ppt TEQ).

The Vietnam-Russia Tropical Center took twenty-four soil samples from Tan Binh commune of Tan Bien District from 1995 to 1998 and found the average dioxin concentration to be 14 ppt TEQ. It also tested seven fish samples, which had an average dioxin level of only 3 ppt TEQ.

The Vietnam-Russia Tropical Center took thirty-nine soil samples in 2000 from Don Thuan commune of Trang Bang District and found dioxin in thirty-two samples, with concentrations ranging from 1.4 to 27.8 ppt TEQ (averaging about 7 ppt TEQ). It also tested six samples of sediments, which revealed dioxin levels from 5.8 to 13.2 ppt TEQ, and one fish sample, which had a dioxin level of 4.2 ppt TEQ.

Ma Da Forest and Tri An Lake, Dong Nai Province

Dong Nai was the most heavily sprayed province of all and was focused on the Ma Da Forest where the famous Military Base D was situated. The total amount of defoliants and herbicides sprayed over Dong Nai Province was reported as 9,440,115 liters, including 4,940,550 liters of Agent Orange. Tri An Lake was created with the construction of the hydropower dam on the Dong Nai River from 1984 to 1987. It is in Vinh Cuu District about 35 kilometers northeast of Bien Hoa City and has a surface area of about 323 square kilometers and a volume of 2,765 billion cubic meters. Tri An Lake is a major source of fresh water for households and irrigation in Dong Nai and Binh Duong Provinces and part of Ho Chi Minh City.

Test results showed the average dioxin concentration in the soil to be 2.2 ppt TEQ, in the sediment at 2.9 ppt TEQ, and in small fish 1.3 ppt TEQ. They could not find dioxin in the four water samples taken.

The 10-80 Committee and Hatfield Consultants in 1997 tested three soil samples from Rang Rang and two sediment samples from Ba Hao Lake and found the dioxin level of soils samples ranging from 2.4 to 20.3 ppt TEQ. The sediment samples had 2.6 and 8 ppt TEQ. Mai Tuan Anh and colleagues did not find TCDD in the seven soil samples they took from Rang Rang area in 2003.

Mangrove forests in Can Gio, Ho Chi Minh City and Ca Mau Province

Can Gio District comprises the estuary of the Saigon River and lies 50 kilometers from the center of Ho Chi Minh City. The Sac Forest in Can Gio was a heavily sprayed area. About 60,232 hectares of the total 105,000 hectares of the forest area were sprayed with 3,776,650 liters of defoliants and herbicides, including 2,149,899 liters of Agent Orange.

Dr. Nguyen Duc Hue of Hanoi National University and the 10-80 Committee tested seven soil samples from Sac Forest. The average level of TCDD was only 16 ppt TEQ (ranging from 0 to 45 ppt TEQ). Matsuda et al. (1993) tested sixteen soil samples from mangrove forests in Ca Mau, where all soil samples exhibited dioxin levels of less than 1 ppt TEQ.

Nha Trang Bay and Saigon River Estuary

To further investigate the transfer of dioxin to the ocean, the Vietnam-Russia Tropical Center tested twenty-four samples of sediments at Nha Trang Bay in Khanh Hoa Province in 2002 and found TCDD in twenty-two samples ranging from 0.1 to 1.2 ppt TEQ. Two of the samples showed TCDD levels of 19.3 and 15.5 ppt TEQ (accounting for 93.0 percent and 86.3 percent TEQ, which means they originated from Agent Orange).

Shiozaki and colleagues (2009) tested five sediment samples from the Saigon River estuary in 2009 and found an average TCDD level of 2.5 ppt TEQ out of a total TEQ of 7.2 ppt. Their five sediment samples upstream in the Saigon River itself averaged less than 0.2 ppt TEQ out of a total TEQ of 1.3 ppt. Because the TCDD levels did not account for a high proportion of their respective total TEQs, the authors concluded that the dioxin in the estuary and river bottom had not originated from Agent Orange.

Former American military bases with dioxin below threshold levels

From 1996 to 1999, the 10-80 Committee and Hatfield Consultants Partnership of Vancouver, Canada, assessed the environmental fate of dioxin residues from the heavy spraying of the Aluoi Valley during the war. Aluoi is about 50 kilometers long north to south and is the westernmost district in Thua Thien-Hue Province, lying along the border with Laos. In the course of the 10-80 Committee's and Hatfield's investigations, it became clear that dioxin levels in the soils and sediments in the valley were well below threshold levels except at the former American base at A So, as reported above.[15]

Based on these findings and the results of other sampling programs the 10-80 Committee and Hatfield conducted in sprayed areas across Vietnam, they proposed that dioxin existed at above-threshold levels primarily, if not exclusively, at other former U.S. military sites.[16] From 2002 to 2006 they evaluated 2,735 locations in southern Vietnam that the United States had used for military facilities, based on available published information and archival research. They progressively narrowed the list to twenty-eight sites with potentially high levels of dioxin. From these they selected eighteen locations that archival information revealed were the framework of Operation Ranch Hand and potentially presented the highest risk to human health. The 10-80/Hatfield scientists visited each of the eighteen locations in 2004 and, on the basis of the information gathered, selected seven for sampling and testing in 2005.

Their study concluded that "Da Nang, Phu Cat and Bien Hoa airfields were identified as significant hot spots on the basis of dioxin levels recorded in soils/sediments." They also analyzed samples from around the perimeters of the airfields at Pleiku, Nha Trang, Can Tho and Tan Son Nhut and inferred that these bases were not likely to be significant hot spots.[17] Their preliminary conclusion has since been confirmed by analyses of samples taken inside these bases by the Ministry of Defense under a United Nations Development Program/Global Environmental Fund (UNDP/GEF) project, the results of which are reported in the following pages.

Former Air Bases at A So, Aluoi and Ta Bat, Thua Thien-Hue Province

In 1996, the 10-80 Committee and Hatfield tested soil samples at these three former U.S. air bases. Two soil samples at A So Air Base had 877 ppt TEQ, the highest levels found. The concentration in other soil samples at A So Air Base was only 94 ppt TEQ. The average level of TCDD in nine samples from Aluoi Air Base was 12 ppt TEQ. The average level of TCDD was 13 ppt in seven samples collected at the former Ta Bat Air Base.[18]

Pleiku Air Base, Gia Lai Province

In 2012, the Office of Committee 33 and the Vietnam-Russia Tropical Center collected seventeen soil samples from Pleiku Air Base at depths up to 40 centimeters. The highest level of TCDD concentration was 5.5 ppt TEQ. Most of the other samples had TCDD levels less than 1 ppt TEQ.[19]

Vam Cong Air Base, An Giang Province

In 2012, the Office of Committee 33 collaborated with the Vietnam-Russia Tropical Center and collected twenty soil samples from Vam Cong Air Base at depths up to 60 centimeters. Most samples had TCDD levels below1 ppt TEQ. The highest level of TCDD concentration was only 1.79 ppt TEQ.

Tan Son Nhat Air Base, Ho Chi Minh City

In 2008, the Vietnam Ministry of National Defense Chemical Command collected twenty-seven soil samples from the loading area for helicopters that were used for spraying. The highest concentration of TCDD was 1,097 ppt TEQ, and the second highest was 643 ppt TEQ, suggesting that other contamination may be present in the area and that further sampling is warranted. Most of the other samples had dioxin levels ranging between 1.1 and 10.0 ppt TEQ.

Phan Rang Air Base, Ninh Thuan Province

In 2008, the Ministry of National Defense Chemical Command tested fifteen soil samples at Phan Rang Air Base. A few of the samples had levels of TCDD of 78.5 ppt TEQ or less. Most of the other samples had dioxin levels at or below 10 ppt TEQ.

Nha Trang Air Base, Khanh Hoa Province

In 2008, the Ministry of National Defense Chemical Command collected three soil samples at depths up to 20 centimeters and one sample at a depth of 30 to 50 centimeters. Dioxin levels of these samples were 50, 23, 22 and 9 ppt TEQ, respectively.

Tuy Hoa Air Base (today Dong Tac Airport), Phu Yen Province

In 2008, the Ministry of National Defense Chemical Command collected four samples from various depths up to 1 meter. The highest level of dioxin found was 38 ppt TEQ. The other samples had dioxin levels of 2.6, 3.7 and 8.6 ppt TEQ.

Dioxin contamination at aircraft crash sites

During the war, aircraft spraying Agent Orange sometimes crashed on takeoff or landing or during their spraying missions. Little is known about the number and locations of such crashes and what became of the herbicide mixtures they were carrying. In 2008–2009, the United States and Vietnam excavated one crash site in Thua Thien-Hue Province. Committee 33 subsequently tested twenty-one soil samples and seventeen sediment samples for dioxin. The highest level of dioxin found was 5.7 ppt TEQ, a level well below Vietnam's threshold level for rural residential use soils.[20]

Three former American military bases with above-threshold levels of dioxin

The air bases at Bien Hoa, Da Nang and Phu Cat were the principal hubs for the Operation Ranch Hand spraying of southern Vietnam and the bases for the C-123 aircraft that were used for this purpose. The three air bases also served as bulk storage and supply facilities for Agent Orange and other Ranch Hand herbicides. The storage sites suffered severe contamination because of the spillage of herbicides and the improper disposal of herbicide barrels, which were rarely completely empty. Dioxin residues accumulated and in the end contaminated 592,300 cubic meters of soil and sediment at these three sites. Eighty-five percent of these soils and sediments are at the Bien Hoa Air Base, 15 percent are at the Da Nang Air Base and 1 percent at Phu Cat. Remediation work has begun.

Bien Hoa Air Base, Dong Nai Province

Bien Hoa Air Base was the largest Operation Ranch Hand site and the dioxin contamination at Bien Hoa is the result of the handling, storage, mixing, loading and spillage of Agent Orange and other herbicides. At Bien Hoa, three large storage tanks were used for herbicide storage — one each for Agent Orange, Agent White and Agent Blue. Additional herbicide formulations also used at the air base included Agents Purple, Pink, Green and others.

According to United States Department of Defense data, the U.S. Army stored 170,000 barrels of herbicides, each containing 55 gallons, or 208 liters, at the base during the course of the war. Of these, 98,000 barrels held Agent Orange, 45,000 barrels had Agent White and 16,000 barrels contained Agent Blue. Agents Purple, Pink, Green and others were also stored at the base. Between December 1969 and March 1970, about 25,000 liters of Agent Orange and 2,500 liters of Agent White entered the soil at Bien Hoa, primarily through leaks from storage tanks. In 1972, U.S. contractors removed approximately 11,000 barrels of Agent Orange and other herbicides under Operation Pacer Ivy. The contents were incinerated near Johnston Island in the eastern Pacific

Ocean in 1978. Given the extensive use and storage of Agent Orange and other herbicides at this site, Bien Hoa Air Base is the largest and most complicated dioxin hot spot.

Since 1990, Vietnam has conducted many projects to assess and analyze the level of dioxin contamination at Bien Hoa. The first soil sample collected was tested for dioxin at the Russian Academy of Sciences and showed a level of TCDD of 59,000 ppt TEQ. In a study in the 1990s, Arnold Schecter reported dioxin levels in soils in Bien Hoa City and the air base that ranged from non-detectable to over 1 million ppt TEQ, but it is not known where the samples were collected.[21] The Ministry of National Defense, the 10-80 Committee and the Office of Committee 33 then carried out more comprehensive studies in collaboration with Hatfield Consultants, funded by the government of Vietnam with the Ford Foundation and then the United Nations Development Program.

The three principal contaminated sites within the air bases are Z1 in the south central part of the base (the former Operation Ranch Hand base), Southwest Area, located west of Z1 near the base boundary (the suspected herbicide storage area for Operation Pacer Ivy) and Pacer Ivy Area on the western end of the air base (used for re-drumming herbicides before export to Johnston Island in the Pacific).

In 2009, the Ministry of National Defense isolated and excavated twenty-three heavily contaminated sites covering 4.7 hectares in the Z1 area. A total of 94,000 cubic meters of soil was contained in a landfill. This included 3,384 cubic meters of soil from three plots that scientists from the Vietnam Academy of Science and Technology treated with a bioremediation technology they have developed.

The topography of the air base generally slopes to the south, and dioxin is most likely carried by runoff to lakes and ponds to the southeast, south and southwest within the city. A study by the Bien Hoa Peoples Committee in 2011 found a concentration of 1,370 ppt TEQ in the sediment of Bien Hung Lake in the city center and 2,752 ppt TEQ in soil in Buu Long ward southwest of the air base.[22] There are twenty lakes on and around the air base, and some are severely contaminated with dioxin. Sediment in one lake in the northeast area tested at 8,900 ppt TEQ. Fat from tilapia fish in the Z1 Lake on the southern edge of the base had a concentration of 1,440 ppt TEQ. Fat from fish taken from the Gate 2 Lake had a concentration of 1,520 ppt TEQ.[23]

In 2012 the Office of Committee 33 collaborated with the Ministry of National Defense and the United Nations Development Program/ Global Environmental Fund to map the boundaries of the hot spots, build a drainage system to capture rainwater runoff from contaminated areas, fence off contaminated land and lakes and place warning signs. They also prepared a master plan for the environmental remediation of Bien Hoa.

In 2016 the Ministry of Defense and the United States Agency for International Development (USAID) completed an environmental assessment of Bien Hoa to identify the extent and depth of dioxin-contaminated soils and sediments, recommend interim mitigation measures and assess strategies and technologies for a major cleanup effort.[24] They collected more than 1,400 samples of soils and sediments — the largest sampling program so far undertaken in Vietnam. Their assessment confirmed dioxin contaminated soils at the Z1, Southwest and Pacer Ivy areas and elevated dioxin concentrations in lake sediments in the Northwest and Northeast areas within the air base and outside the air base at Gate 2 Lake, Bien Hung Lake and in the drainage canal west of the Pacer Ivy Area. In the map of the Bien Hoa Air Base on page 114, the red hatchings are the locations of dioxin contamination identified in previous studies and confirmed by the USAID study. The yellow lines delineate the known and potential areas of dioxin contamination.[25]

Applying the Vietnamese threshold levels for dioxin contamination, the 2016 assessment produced estimates of the volume of dioxin-contaminated soils and sediments requiring treatment.

Table 1.3. Contaminated Soils and Sediments in Bien Hoa

	Baseline Volume (m3)	Baseline with Contingency Volume (m3)
Soils	315,700	377,700
Sediments	92,800	117,600
Total	408.500	495,300

The total volume of soil and sediment to be treated at Bien Hoa is 495,300 cubic meters. This estimate includes a contingency factor to cover the possibility of more dioxin being discovered in the course of a future remediation project. The study then estimated the cost to treat 495,300 cubic meters of soil and sediments using different techniques and combinations of techniques. Three of these techniques, their estimated costs and the time needed to implement each of them are shown in the table below. Actual costs may vary as shown in the table below, depending on the amount of material that ultimately requires treatment and the time required to complete the remediation project.[26]

Table 1.4. Cost Estimates and Time Required to Remediate Soils & Sediments in Bien Hoa

Technique	Estimated Cost (USD Millions)	Range		Years to Completion
		-40% (USD Millions)	+75% (USD Millions)	
Passive Landfill	$137	$82	$239	8-11
Thermal Conductive Heating	$640	$384	$1,121	17-21
Incineration	$794	$476	$1,389	11-15

Passive landfill is the least costly technique. It requires the collection and long-term storage without treatment of all contaminated soils and sediments. Thermal conductive heating and incineration destroy dioxin by heating contaminated soils and sediments to very high temperatures. Thermal conductive heating, also known by its proprietary name of In-pile Thermal Desorption, is the technique used to remediate the Da Nang Airport. Incineration is the most expensive technology. It could cost $800 million or as much as $1.4 billion and take eleven to fifteen years.[27]

Remediating the dioxin in Bien Hoa will be costly and complicated. Vietnam and the United States have not decided which technology to use, nor have the two governments identified sources of funding. Given the high costs for remediation, a combination of technologies may be employed, and the work may be conducted in phases.

In the meantime, the government of Vietnam must stop people from raising, selling and eating dioxin-contaminated fish from the sixteen lakes and ponds in and around the Bien Hoa Air Base. Investigations in 2009 and 2011, cited in the 2016 environmental assessment, have documented that whole fish, fish fat and fish muscle from these lakes and ponds contain dioxin at levels that exceed Vietnamese standards. Dioxin has also been found in blood serum and breast milk in the people living in Bien Hoa. The highest concentrations are found in people who regularly consume tilapia and other fish species from the air base.[28] Despite information campaigns, fencing and warning signs and an official ban on fishing enacted in 2010, people in Bien Hoa continue to fish and practice aquaculture in and around the air base.

The government of Vietnam, in particular the Ministry of Defense and the Bien Hoa Peoples Committee, should immediately collect and destroy fish, ducks and other aquatic animals in all lakes on the air base and all dioxin-contaminated lakes outside the air base and prevent their reintroduction.

Da Nang Airport

Da Nang Airport was one of the key Operation Ranch Hand sites and was second only to Bien Hoa in terms of number of C-123 spray missions and volume of herbicides stored and used. The U.S. military stored 94,900 barrels of defoliants and herbicides, including 52,700 barrels of Agent Orange. During Operation Pacer Ivy, it stored 8,220 barrels of Agent Orange. There have also been multiple incidents of leakage, resulting in severe contamination of the soil.

The Vietnam-Russia Tropical Center conducted the earliest research on dioxin residues at the Da Nang airport in 1995. Subsequent studies were conducted by the 10-80 Committee (2003–2005) and the Office of Committee 33 (2006 and 2009) in collaboration with Hatfield Consultants and funded by the Ford Foundation. In 2006 Vietnam started to cooperate with the U.S. Environmental Protection Agency in investigating dioxin contamination. The studies found dioxin concentrations exceeding the threshold level in the areas where the spray planes were loaded and where the herbicide was mixed, as well as the former herbicide drum storage area and in Sen Lake, downstream from these two locations. The samples that exceeded the allowable standard are shown as red or orange dots in the map on page 116. The dioxin levels in soil and sediment samples outside the airport were below the allowable limits. These areas therefore do not require remediation.[29]

Based on the 2003–2005 and 2006 studies, in early 2007 the Ford Foundation funded the Office of Committee 33 and the Ministry of Defense to immobilize the most contaminated soil with a heavy concrete slab covering the former Ranch Hand mixing and loading area, to construct interim facilities to capture and treat rainwater runoff containing contaminated sediments, to construct an airport perimeter fence to stop further public access to the hot spot and to end all fishing and agriculture in and around Sen Lake at the north end of the airport. Results from the 2009 study suggested that these interim mitigation measures reduced the potential dioxin exposure pathways for people living near the north end of the Da Nang airport.[30]

Drawing on this experience, USAID conducted an environmental impact assessment for Da Nang during in 2010-2011. On August 9, 2012, USAID and the Ministry of National Defense of Vietnam broke ground on a project to clean up 72,900 cubic meters of contaminated soil and sediment at Da Nang Air Base. They chose a remediation technology called in-pile thermal desorption, which heats the soil to 330 degrees Celsius inside a containment structure. Worker safety issues were addressed by mandatory use of personal protective equipment. The project was originally scheduled to be completed in 2016. However, the amounts of contaminated sediment from the drainage ditch and adjacent wetlands were significantly larger than originally estimated. The amounts of dioxin in the wastewater and fumes from the thermal desorption technology were also larger than expected, and 240 tons of activated carbon were needed to remove it. The activated carbon has since been shipped out of Vietnam to Switzerland for treatment and disposal. For these reasons the remediation of the dioxin at the airport has taken longer than originally thought, and costs have increased. The facility at the Da Nang Airport is scheduled to treat its last round of dioxin-contaminated soils in late 2017 and be decommissioned in 2018. In the end, the project remediated 90,000 cubic meters of contaminated soils and sediments. The total cost is now expected to be $108 million.

In sum, the Da Nang project is both complex and the first to be done at such a scale in Vietnam. It is not uncommon for very large cleanup projects in other countries, including the United States, to underestimate the volume of contaminated materials and the cost and time required to remediate them.

Phu Cat Air Base

Phu Cat Air Base is in a rural area of Binh Dinh Province, about 50 kilometers northwest of the provincial capital, Qui Nhon. The air base was used to store 28,900 barrels of defoliants and herbicides, including 17,000 barrels of Agent Orange. Beginning in 1999, Vietnam investigated dioxin residues at the air base and found the area contaminated with dioxin to be about 2,000 square meters. The highest concentration of dioxin just below the topsoil was 11,400 ppt TEQ; at a depth of 60 centimeters it was 1,456 ppt TEQ and at 90 centimeters it was 926 ppt TEQ.

With additional data from the U.S. Department of Defense on Operation Pacer Ivy, the Office of Committee 33, together with the Vietnam-Russia Tropical Center and Hatfield Consultants, carried out further research and identified an additional 400 square meters of dioxin-contaminated area, with an average level of 3,000 ppt TEQ. Some samples were as high as 89,879 ppt TEQ. In several lakes on the air base, the level of dioxin in the sediment ranged from non-detectable levels to 127 ppt TEQ.

In 2012, the Office of Committee 33 and the Ministry of National Defense removed 7,000 square meters of dioxin-contaminated soil to a landfill at a remote site on the air base and used passive landfill technology to secure the site. The United Nations Development Program/Global Environmental Facility funded the landfill. The Czech Republic paid Dekonta, a company based in that country, to provide equipment and training for Ministry of Defense staff at Phu Cat so they can continue to monitor the landfill. The landfill should be monitored every six months to ensure that no dioxin is escaping from the site.

The following table summarizes the status of the three dioxin hot spots.[31]

Table 1.5. Dioxin Contamination at the Three Agent Orange / Dioxin Hot Spots in Vietnam

	Bien Hoa	Da Nang	Phu Cat
Highest recorded levels of dioxin:			
in Soil	962,559 ppt TEQ	365,000 ppt TEQ	238,000 ppt TEQ
in Sediment	5,970 ppt TEQ	8,580 ppt TEQ	201 ppt TEQ
Total volume of contaminated soil & sediment	495,300 m³	90,000 m³	7,000 m³
Cleanup technology	To be selected	In-pile Thermal Desorption	Passive landfill
Cost of clean up (foreign contribution)	$800 million (incineration)	$112 million (projected)	$5 million
Cleanup completion date	2030	2018	2011
Cooperating agencies	MOD & USAID	MOD & USAID	MOD/MONRE & UNDP/GEF

Among the three hot spots, the maximum soil dioxin TEQ was greatest at the Bien Hoa Air Base: 800 times the Vietnamese maximum acceptable level of 1,200 ppt TEQ. Soil dioxin TEQs at the other two sites exceeded this level by 200 to 300 times. Bien Hoa is by far the largest dioxin hot spot, with the volume of contaminated soils and sediments there five times that of Da Nang and Phu Cat combined.

Dioxin and the Food Chain in Da Nang and Bien Hoa

The 10-80 Committee and Hatfield Consultants demonstrated without doubt the food chain transfer of TCDD from contaminated soil to fish pond sediments to fish and duck tissues and then to humans as measured in whole blood and breast milk in their original study of the Aluoi Valley and in subsequent studies at the Da Nang and Bien Hoa Air Bases.[32] Tables 1.7 and 1.8 on page 41 summarize their findings for the presence of TCDD in people who were living around the former A So Air Base in 1999–2001.

Studies conducted in 2009 on tilapia from Sen Lake at the Da Nang Airport found contaminant concentrations in fish fat as high as 8,350 ppt TEQ, and other high readings in fish muscle (88.2 ppt TEQ), eggs (1,290 ppt TEQ) and liver (1,540 ppt TEQ), which all exceeded a Health Canada threshold of 20 ppt TEQ. In 2006, tilapia fat tissues analyzed from Sen Lake also showed very high TEQ values (3,120 ppt). Fish sampled from the rest of the lakes and ponds inside the Da Nang Airport generally remained below the Health Canada threshold.[33] Sen Lake has since been drained and its contaminated fish and sediments have been treated as part of the Da Nang airport remediation project.

A study in 2010 found concentrations of TCDD in Bien Hoa Air Base tilapia consistent with those reported for Da Nang. Tilapia sampled from all lakes and ponds inside and outside the air base had concentrations in fat tissue that exceeded applicable U.S. and international guidelines. The highest recorded level in fish fat was 4,040 ppt TEQ.[34] The proper way to protect the health of the public in Bien Hoa is to stop human consumption of tilapia as well as of other fish and aquatic animals, including ducks and snails, that are being raised and caught on the Bien Hoa Air Base. However, air base authorities have been slow to end the rearing and marketing of ducks and fish.

More than 90 percent of the human exposure to dioxins comes through the consumption of contaminated food. In the Vietnam context this means fish, ducks, snails and other aquatic animals living in contaminated ponds and lakes. Dioxins are lipophilic and tend to be stored in fatty tissues with the result that the chemicals build up in blood and breast tissue and milk during lactation. Breast-fed infants are the most vulnerable part of the human population: the concentration of dioxin in breast milk can deliver more dioxin to an infant per kilo of body weight than children and adults get from other sources.

Many countries have taken a standards/guideline approach to protect human health from dioxin exposure. Studies in Da Nang and Bien Hoa in 2009 and 2010 applied these guidelines to assessing dioxin levels in human blood and breast milk.

Table 1.6. Dioxin Threshold Levels

Level of Dioxin in:	Guideline Amount	Explanation
Whole blood	3-7 pg/g (lipid) TCDD	3-7 pg/gram is the typical range in the general population of industrialized countries and rarely exceeds 10pg/g
Blood serum	30 ppt TEQ	30 ppt is equivalent to a chronic intake of 4 pg/kg/day
Breast milk	30 ppt TEQ	30 ppt is equivalent to the WHO Tolerable Daily Intake guideline of 4 pg TEQ/kg body weight/day

The studies documented elevated dioxin levels in airport workers, fishermen and people consuming fish cultivated on the airport grounds as summarized in the following two tables.[35]

Table 1.7. Dioxin Concentrations in Human Blood (Da Nang and Bien Hoa)

Da Nang			Bien Hoa		
Average Concentrations across Samples					
101 whole blood samples - 2009			42 blood serum samples - 2009		
	TCDD ppt	TEQ ppt		TCDD ppt	TEQ ppt
Mean	59	96.4	Mean	181.5	197.9
Median	10.4	50.7	Median	67.75	82.9
Five Highest Concentrations of Dioxin in Individuals					
	TCDD ppt	TEQ ppt		TCDD ppt	TEQ ppt
Male	1340	1410	Male	1970	2020
Male	1150	1220	Female	1130	1150
Female	785	893	Male	1040	1080
Female	589	696	Male	327	347
Female	567	662	Male	322	343

Whole blood dioxin (TCDD) levels from Da Nang residents ranged from a minimum of 1.7 to 1,340 ppt TCDD and well over a majority had levels that exceeded the threshold. Working on the airport significantly increased blood TCDD and TEQ and many samples showed a high ratio of TCDD to TEQ, indicating the dioxin originated from Agent Orange or other herbicides. Serum dioxin levels for Bien Hoa air base workers ranged from 19.3 to 2,020 pg/g lipid basis. TEQ concentrations in all but one sample exceeded the WHO standard of 30 ppt. The three highest levels of TEQ were found in individuals who harvest fish and lotus plants from the Bien Hoa Air Base. Their dioxin levels were more than 35 times the threshold level.

Table 1.8. Dioxin Concentrations in Human Breast Milk (Da Nang and Bien Hoa)

Da Nang			Bien Hoa		
Average Concentrations across Samples					
15 samples- 2009			22 samples- 2010		
	TCDD ppt	TEQ ppt		TCDD ppt	TEQ ppt
Mean	22.2	39.1	Mean	6.5	11.6
Median	5.1	20.8	Median	2.7	7.5
Five Highest Concentrations of Dioxin in Individuals					
	TCDD ppt	TEQ ppt		TCDD ppt	TEQ ppt
Female	232	263	Female	30.3	39.6
Female	24.4	53.2	Female	13.8	31.8
Female	23.6	45.8	Female	22.5	28.6
Female	6.76	42.4	Female	9.85	14
Female	7.0	29.8	Female	<12.3	13.7

All breast milk samples exhibited TEQs that exceeded the World Health Organization's Tolerable Daily Intake guideline of 4 pg TEQ/kg body weight/day. On average, the TCDD concentrations in breast milk samples from Da Nang were higher than the samples analyzed from Bien Hoa. A milk sample from a Da Nang Air Base worker had the highest level of dioxin — 232 ppt TCDD (263 ppt TEQ). She had consumed fish laden with dioxin from the sediments in Sen Lake on the north end of the Da Nang airport. The maximum level in Bien Hoa — 30.3 ppt TCDD (39.6 ppt TEQ) — was detected in a twenty-nine-year-old mother who was breast-feeding her second child.

Dioxin from other sources

In 2012–2013, the Office of Committee 33 collaborated with the Vietnam-Russia Tropical Center and the Dioxin Laboratory of the Vietnam Environment Administration to do research on dioxin emissions at a number of cement and steel factories and several waste treatment plants.[36] The results showed that in some of the areas investigated, the amount of dioxin in wastewater and in the atmosphere exceeded the allowed standard, sometimes substantially.

In Bien Hoa, Nguyen Hung Minh and colleagues researched the emission of dioxin in 2015 from two industrial waste treatment plants.[37] The samples of emitted fume were collected using the isokinetic technique, consistent to Method 23 of the U.S. Environmental Protection Agency. Fly ash samples were collected from the dust-gathering units. Wastewater samples were collected from the aerated water treatment tanks (no disposal). Some soil samples from near the waste treatment plant were also collected for dioxin testing.

The researchers found that dioxin levels in the air emitted at one of the waste treatment plants ranged from 10.3 to 34.4 ng TEQ/Nm³, the concentration of polychlorinated dibenzodioxins (PCDDs) and polychlorinated dibenzofurans (PCDFs) in gas emissions, expressed as nanograms (ng) of dioxin toxic equivalent (TEQ) per normal cubic meter (Nm³). The level at the other plant ranged from 0.967 to 4.95 ng TEQ/Nm³. Both these levels are higher than the permitted levels in both Vietnam (1.2 ng TEQ/Nm³) and the European Union (0.1 ng TEQ/Nm³). Soil samples at the plants had an average dioxin level of 391 ng/kg. In fly ash samples, the level of dioxin was as high as 2,755 ng TEQ/kg, which also exceeds Vietnamese standards.

Nguyen Hung Minh and colleagues also analyzed samples of plant air emissions from a steam-generating incinerator at a Bien Hoa paper factory.[38] The result was that the level of dioxin in the air emissions was 0.4 to 1.1 ng/TEQ/Nm³ (lower than Vietnamese standard), the level of dioxin in furnace treatment water was 0.148 to 0.156 ng/TEQ/L and the level of dioxin in the produced dust was relatively low at 38.8 ng/TEQ/kg.

Similar studies were carried out in Da Nang. Research showed that the dioxin levels at the waste treatment facility in Da Nang ranged from 5.1 to 7.5 ng/TEQ/Nm³, exceeding the Vietnamese standard. In soil samples collected here, the level of dioxin varied from 316 to 583 TEQ/g.

Another study by Committee 33 in areas that were never sprayed with Agent Orange found levels of dioxin in chicken and pork that exceeded allowable levels in the European Union.[39] Though still small in number, such studies provide strong warnings of dioxin contamination from other sources in Vietnam.

Nguyen Hung Minh and colleagues in 2014 also studied the difference between dioxin originated from defoliants and herbicides and dioxin from other sources. The key difference was that the proportion of TCDD in defoliant and herbicide dioxin samples was at a high or very high level (50 percent to 90 percent).[40]

Dioxin management in Vietnam

The establishment of the 10-80 Committee in 1980 and the Office of the National Steering Committee for the Overcoming of the Consequences of Toxic Chemicals Used by USA in the War in Vietnam (Committee 33) in 1999 demonstrated the concern and commitment of Vietnam in researching and treatment of the effects of defoliant dioxin. In 2004, Vietnam joined the Stockholm Convention on Persistent Organic Pollutants (POPs).

In June 2014, the Vietnam National Assembly approved the Law on Environment Protection, which took effect from January 1, 2015. Article 61, Item 4 provides that: "Land areas containing soil and sediment exposed to the dioxin agent which is derived from the herbicide used in the war time, remains of plant pesticides and other hazardous substances must be investigated, assessed, restricted and disposed in order to meet the required standards set out in the environmental protection regulations." The law directs the government to provide detailed regulations on this issue, and this task has been assigned to the Ministry of Natural Resources and Environment. The ministry is to take the lead and coordinate other ministries and provincial People's Committees to organize research and recovery from the consequences of the defoliants and herbicides, as specified in the decree on the organization, mandates and functions of the Ministry of Natural Resources and Environment.

Vietnam now has two high-standard dioxin testing laboratories, with results cross-checked by dioxin testing laboratories in Germany and Japan. The two laboratories are the Dioxin Laboratory of the Vietnam Environment Administration, which was built with funding from the Bill and Melinda Gates Foundation and Atlantic Philanthropies, and the Dioxin Laboratory at the Vietnam-Russia Tropical Center. Several other research, training and service centers in Hanoi, Ho Chi Minh City and Can Tho are also equipped with modern facilities for dioxin testing.

Who Has Been Exposed to Agent Orange/Dioxin, and How Many Victims of Agent Orange Are There in Vietnam?

Not everyone who was living in the sprayed areas was exposed to dioxin, nor is it possible to definitively enumerate the individuals who were exposed or know the frequency, duration and intensity of their exposure, the resulting levels of dioxin in their bodies or the consequences for their future health and offspring. For these reasons, it is impossible to determine the actual numbers of Agent Orange victims in in Vietnam. Nevertheless, at the population level we see the consequences of dioxin for the Vietnamese in terms of ill health, shortened lives and birth defects. Some 10 percent to 15 percent of all Vietnamese with disabilities are Agent Orange victims. They are primarily living with mobility impairments and mental disabilities rather than hearing, vision or speech problems. Their disabilities affect them severely.

Consideration of these questions must begin with several facts.

- Agent Orange and several other herbicides contaminated with dioxin were brought to Vietnam by the United States

and used there and in adjacent border areas in Laos and Cambodia during the Vietnam war. Little is known about the spraying in
these neighboring countries. In Vietnam there are different figures on the total amount of dioxin dispersed. The lowest figure,
estimated by Jeanne Mager Stellman and colleagues, is 366 kilograms of dioxin.[1]

- The dioxin levels in the blood of people living in heavily sprayed
  areas of the south (Da Nang and Thua Thien-Hue) were significantly higher than levels in people living in the north (Hai
  Phong).[2]

- The dioxin residue in the blood and breast milk of those who
  were exposed to it at the former American air bases at Da Nang
  and Bien Hoa is of the type found in Agent Orange and several
  of the other herbicides that were used; the source of the dioxin
  has been confirmed to be from Agent Orange and several of the
  color-coded herbicides.[3]

- Dioxins are some of the most toxic substances that humans have
  ever discovered or created.

- Research institutes in Vietnam and the United States have carried out several epidemiological studies on the possible effects
  of dioxin exposure on human populations. In the Vietnam study
  of 47,000 war veterans, the incidence of diseases in those with
  a history of high exposure to dioxin was found to be statistically significant compared to the control group with no history
  of exposure to dioxin.[4] The U.S. Air Force Health Study compared morbidity, mortality and reproductive health outcomes
  from 1982 to 2002 for 1,047 servicemen who conducted spraying missions under Operation Ranch Hand with 1,223 Air
  Force crew and maintenance staff who flew C-130 aircraft elsewhere in Southeast Asia from 1962 to 1971. The study found
  little evidence of a connection between serum dioxin levels and
  increased morbidity. It did show an increased risk of mortality
  from all causes for Ranch Hand participants, particularly ground
  crew, relative to the group of other Air Force personnel.[5]

Scientific studies have not yet explained the physiological processes within the body by which dioxin may lead to diseases, often later in life, or birth defects in following generations. At the level of the individual case, we cannot confirm that the diseases are caused by dioxin. However, future research may further develop our understanding.

For example, the Institute of Genome Research, directed by Associate Professor Nong Van Hai of the Vietnam Academy of Science and Technology, carried out some research projects on gene mutations in people with elevated dioxin concentrations in the blood from 2000 to 2015. Professor Hai and his colleagues have detected changes in Genes P53, Cyp1A1, AhR and MSH2 in the families of the veterans who have a history of exposure to dioxin. (They lived in areas sprayed with Agent Orange and had elevated levels of dioxin in the blood.) In the five family histories they studied, they found 17 mutations in Gene P53, 8 mutations in Gene Cyp1A1, 31 mutations in Gene AhR 31 and 6 mutations in Gene MSH 2-E13. These mutations alter the amino acids related to some cancers.

This is a new discovery of gene mutations in people exposed to dioxin, but people can ask the question whether there are other factors (physical, chemical or biological) that can cause similar mutations and whether we have excluded these factors. The answer is deadlocked: We are not sure about the scientific evidence about the harmful effects of dioxin on these people. Dioxin and ill health is similar to the case of cigarettes and disease, although dioxin is much more toxic than the chemicals found in cigarette tobacco. Tobacco companies are required to print warnings on cigarette packages that smoking causes lung cancer and heart disease. But there are cases of people with lung cancer who never smoked and of those who smoke but have never gotten lung cancer. Therefore, the determination of victims of Agent Orange needs to follow the methods used for showing that use of tobacco causes lung cancer.

Dioxin from Agent Orange or any other source can enter the human body in four ways: through the digestive tract from eating certain foods contaminated with dioxin, by inhaling dioxin-laden dust, through the skin if it is broken and, for infants, by ingesting breast milk from a mother who has absorbed dioxin through one of the first three routes. Of these four routes, the first — exposure from eating dioxin-contaminated foods — is the most common.

People who were living in the areas sprayed with Agent Orange during the 1960s or who later worked on or lived near a handful of former U.S. military air bases may have been exposed to dioxin in the soil or acquired it by eating food grown in nearby dioxin-contaminated soils or ponds. If food from these areas were sold elsewhere, those consumers could also be exposed. Moreover, people who live downstream of the sprayed areas could still be affected by dioxin-contaminated sediments mobilized during heavy monsoon rains and transported downstream. All these factors mean that it is difficult to specify with any certainty who may have been exposed.

Moreover, simple residence in the provinces that were sprayed at the time of the spraying is not certain proof of exposure. Proof would require substantiation that dioxin contaminated the environment in a particular locale and that the level of dioxin was sufficient to affect the health of the people living there. It is not possible today to measure dioxin concentrations that may have existed in the soil and in food in Vietnam a half century ago. Historical data with such broad coverage do not exist. Moreover, it is not feasible to collect such kinds of data in every locality in Vietnam today.

In consequence, to claim that everyone living in the sprayed areas before 1972, or 1975, was exposed has no scientific basis. The definition of who was exposed to dioxin is thus a very broad one. For example, the U.S. Department of Veterans Affairs considers that all American veterans who were anywhere in the south of Vietnam between 1961 and 1975 and who later developed a listed disease or medical condition are presumed to have been exposed. This definition of presumed exposure is both pragmatic and humane.

Some people believe that blood samples must be analyzed for dioxin to determine who has been exposed. This is only true for those who have been recently exposed to dioxin. Although many people were exposed to dioxin in the 1960s, the body gradually eliminates it. The half-life of dioxin is 7.6 years,[6] meaning that half of it is gone from the body within this period. The remaining concentration gradually decreases to low or undetectable levels, but the effects of dioxin in the body remain. Therefore, a person may have been exposed to dioxin in the past, but a blood test today might not indicate it, or might suggest the exposure was lower than it actually was.

A study of people in Da Nang who had been exposed to dioxin showed that the concentration of dioxin in the blood has no correlation with the incidence of disease. There are people who have low levels of dioxin but have typical dioxin-related diseases, such as lymphoma and prostate cancer. There are also people who have very high levels of dioxin but are leading healthy lives. For example, a woman who raised and consumed fish from the dioxin-contaminated lake inside the Da Nang Airport was measured with a very high blood dioxin level of 1,220 ppt TEQ. She, however, showed no signs of disease; she was exposed but healthy. The duration of exposure and a robust immune system may be factors in such cases.[7]

Doctors use typical symptoms, backed up by biological tests, to evaluate cases of people who may have been exposed to toxic chemicals. However, in the case of dioxin toxicity, doctors cannot find such typical or specific symptoms, nor are there specific biological tests. Diagnosis therefore must rely on showing exposure to dioxin and excluding other causes. Medical researchers must then turn to epidemiological studies and compare the incidence of diseases between exposed populations with non-exposed populations to establish a relationship at the population level.

With the research and diagnostic capabilities in medicine available today, we can only diagnose dioxin toxicity on the basis of answers to two questions: Did the patient have the opportunity to be exposed to dioxin? Is the patient's illness or condition on the list of diseases and conditions associated with exposure to dioxin? These two criteria are both practical and humane, and both Vietnam and the U.S. currently use them. Even so, they may miss certain genuine cases because exposure is unknown or causality has not been established.

In 2008 Vietnam's Ministry of Health issued a list of the diseases, deformities and disabilities related to exposure to toxic chemicals/ dioxin.[8] The Ministry of Health list is primarily based on the list of veterans' diseases associated with Agent Orange that the U.S. Department of Veterans Affairs issued in the 1990s and has updated every two years since then. Each agency also shows diseases and conditions that do not appear in the other agency's list, as shown here.

Table 2.1. Diseases & Conditions Associated with Exposure to Dioxin, Recognized by both Vietnam and the U.S.

Vietnam Ministry of Health - 2008	U.S. Department of Veterans Affairs - 2015	Description
1. Soft tissue sarcoma	Soft tissue sarcomas (other than osteosarcoma, chondrosarcoma, Kaposi's sarcoma, or mesothelioma)	A group of different types of cancers in body tissues such as muscle, fat, blood and lymph vessels, and connective tissues
2. Non-Hodgkin's lymphoma	Non-Hodgkin's lymphoma	A group of cancers that affect the lymph glands and other lymphatic tissue
3. Hodgkin's disease	Hodgkin's disease	A malignant lymphoma (cancer) characterized by progressive enlargement of the lymph nodes, liver, and spleen, and by progressive anemia
4. Lung and bronchus cancer	Respiratory cancers (includes lung cancer)	Cancers of the lung, larynx, trachea and bronchus
5. Trachea cancer	*(See above)*	*(See above)*
6. Larynx cancer	*(See above)*	*(See above)*
7. Prostate cancer	Prostate cancer	Cancer of the prostate; one of the most common cancers among men
8. Primary liver cancer	AL amyloidosis	A rare disease caused when an abnormal protein, amyloid, enters tissues or organs
9. Kahler's disease	Multiple myeloma	A cancer of plasma cells, a type of white blood cell in bone marrow
10. Acute and subacute peripheral neuropathy	Peripheral neuropathy, early onset	A nervous system condition that causes numbness, tingling and motor weakness. Under U.S. rating regulations, it must be at least 10 percent disabling within one year of herbicide exposure
11. Spina bifida	Spina bifida (except spina bifida occulta)	A defect in the developing fetus that results in incomplete closing of the spine
12. Chloracne	Chloracne (or similar acneform disease)	A skin condition that occurs soon after exposure to chemicals and looks like common forms of acne seen in teenagers. Under U.S. rating regulations, it must be at least 10 percent disabling within one year of exposure to herbicides.
13. Type 2 diabetes	Diabetes Mellitus Type 2	A disease characterized by high blood sugar levels resulting from the body's inability to respond properly to the hormone insulin
14. Porphyria cutanea tarda	Porphyria cutanea tarda	A disorder characterized by liver dysfunction and by thinning and blistering of the skin in sun-exposed areas. Under U.S. rating regulations, it must be at least 10 percent disabling within one year of exposure to herbicides.

Table 2.2. Diseases & Conditions Associated with Exposure to Dioxin, Recognized by EITHER Vietnam OR the U.S., but Not Both

Recognized ONLY by the Vietnam Ministry of Health (NOT by U.S. Veterans Affairs)	Recognized ONLY by the U.S. Department of Veterans Affairs (NOT by Vietnam Ministry of Health)
Unusual births	Chronic B-cell leukemias
Deformities and birth defects	Ischemic heart disease
Mental disorders	Parkinson's disease

In 2015, the U.S. Department of Veterans Affairs paid $23.7 billion in disability compensation to 1,347,433 veterans who served in the armed forces during the Vietnam era and subsequently applied for benefits, a payment of $17,600 per person.[9] Of these, 527,925 were veterans with one of the above diseases or conditions associated with exposure to Agent Orange while they were in Vietnam.[10]

When people ask about the consequences of Agent Orange in Vietnam, one of their first questions is "How many people are affected?" This is not a simple question, and the answers given are often very different. In fact, it is impossible to determine a specific and fixed number — to do so would first require one to confirm the actual numbers of people exposed to dioxin. This cannot be done because of many unknowns — the actual day-to-day exposure of people on the ground to spraying operations over large areas over nine years, the half-life of dioxin under different environmental conditions and the dispersion of dioxin in the environment, both from the spraying and the dioxin hot spots. But even if exposure to dioxin could be proved with certainty, the illnesses and birth defects linked to dioxin also have other causes, and even diagnosing them correctly in large numbers of people requires expertise and facilities not typically available throughout the country. Therefore, it is impossible to confirm the number of Agent Orange victims in Vietnam. This parallels the challenges in determining the number of Agent Orange victims among U.S. veterans and veterans of the American allies who joined the war in Vietnam.

Nevertheless there have been efforts over the years to count the numbers of victims of Agent Orange in Vietnam.

In 2000, Professor Hoang Dinh Cau, former deputy minister of health and chairman of the 10-80 Committee,[11] the government panel in charge of Agent Orange/dioxin research in Vietnam, estimated that there were about 1 million Agent Orange victims, including about 150,000 children with birth defects. These estimates were subsequently much quoted. However, his report did not explain his methods or how he arrived at these figures.[12]

In 2003, Jeanne Mager Stellman, now professor emerita of health policy and management at Columbia University, and her colleagues independently published their analysis of the herbicide spraying using U.S. Department of Defense records and maps and data on population and residential patterns in Vietnam in the 1960s. They said: "Among the hamlets with some population data, 3,181 were sprayed directly and at least 2.1 million but perhaps as many as 4.8 million people would have been present during the spraying."[13] To an unknown degree, these numbers are underestimates since they do not include soldiers of both sides and other transients who were on the ground at the time nor do they include Laos and Cambodia. These are estimates of exposure in the 1960s. People continue to ask how many Agent Orange victims there are today.

In its first five-year research program, Committee 33 assigned this question to the Ministry of Labor, Invalids and Social Affairs (MOLISA), and the ministry set out to identify and enumerate the number of victims of Agent Orange throughout the country. Ministry guidelines stipulated that victims should be able to show they had lived in a sprayed area and that they were currently suffering from one or more of the illnesses on a list provided by the Ministry of Health. MOLISA completed the enumeration in 2005, and it showed about 500,000 Agent Orange victims at that time.[14] At a meeting to review the report, some officials believed this was an underestimate because of the reluctance of many Vietnamese to be identified as Agent Orange victims. Many people, the officials felt, worried that such a label could adversely affect the psychology of their children and their prospects for marriage and children of their own.

Public attention to the Agent Orange legacy ramped up in 2006–2007 as a result of media reports about foreign nongovernmental organizations assisting children and young adults with disabilities linked to dioxin, as well as from Ford Foundation and Dialogue Group press conferences, attention from United Nations agencies, positive actions by the U.S. Embassy and fresh research findings from Committee 33. These developments led top officials in the government of Vietnam to pay more attention to the issue. Agent Orange victims and their families as well as the Vietnam Association of Victims of Agent Orange spoke up and asked for help. The Government expanded its monthly allowance explicitly for Agent Orange victims, and as a result the numbers of people who registered as victims increased rapidly. However, between a third and half of such registrants later proved to not meet the program criteria. The Vietnamese government has now strengthened its procedures and specified the required documentation for considering the recognition of victims. Nevertheless, controversies and difficulties persist in the identification of victims. There are still abuses of policies that were designed to benefit the victims. There are people recognized as victims who are not actually victims. Some victims are not recognized as such because they lack the required documentation or are otherwise outside the boundaries of the current benefits program.

Thus, even the number of current beneficiaries cannot be taken as the total number of Agent Orange victims in Vietnam.

It is possible to approximate the numbers of people who may have been affected by dioxin-contaminated defoliants like Agent Orange. They may have been affected because their parents or grandparents (or possibly even their great-grandparents) were directly exposed to the spraying itself. Or a parent may have been living in close proximity to a dioxin hot spot at a former American air base. We focus here on the disabilities that begin with birth defects linked to indirect exposure to dioxin, rather than on the health consequences for those who were directly exposed — cancers, Hodgkin's disease, chloracne, Parkinson's disease, porphyria cutanea tarda, ischemic heart disease, hypertension, Type 2 diabetes and others.

The 2009 Vietnam Population and Household Census (hereinafter VPHC)[15] estimates that there are 6.1 million disabled people in Vietnam. The Vietnamese, however, are not asking the United States to assist all people with disabilities. They are asking for help only for Agent Orange victims, a subset of the total number of Vietnamese with disabilities. The government of Vietnam does not assert that everyone with disabilities in Vietnam is an "Agent Orange victim." It applies that term to individuals, but only after they have met certain specific criteria.[16]

Who are the Agent Orange victims in Vietnam? Over the last eight years the Vietnam Red Cross and VAVA have sought to answer this question through various surveys in districts and provinces around the country. However, for many reasons it has proved challenging to compile these data into a full picture of a particular province. The one exception is Da Nang.

In each of Da Nang's seven districts in 2006, officials assembled personal information and health and disability status on 7,000 people they considered to be victims of Agent Orange. In 2007, the Da Nang branch of the Vietnam Association of Victims of Agent Orange/Dioxin sent teams to the homes of each of the 7,000. The teams reviewed personal histories and types of health and disability issues against two criteria: potential exposure and whether the person's condition appeared on the list that the Ministry of Health had released of illnesses and conditions associated with dioxin.[17] The VAVA teams concluded that 5,077 people in Da Nang met these two criteria.

These data can be used to begin to paint a picture of who the Vietnamese consider to be Agent Orange victims. In the first quarter of 2014, the Aspen Institute's Agent Orange in Vietnam Program selected four of Da Nang's districts[18] and examined the records of everyone deemed an Agent Orange victim. Three of these districts, Thanh Khe, Hai Chau and Cam Le, surround the Da Nang airport. The airport contains a major dioxin hot spot, the focus of a U.S.-funded remediation project. The fourth district is Da Nang's rural hinterland, Hoa Vang. Hoa Vang covers the largely mountainous western part of the city and was chosen for its possible similarity to more remote rural districts in other provinces that were heavily sprayed.

This analysis focuses on people whose disabilities are linked to indirect exposure to dioxin — that is, the offspring of those who were directly exposed. The U.S. military started using Agent Orange in then-South Vietnam in 1962 but nearly all the herbicides (97.3 percent) that were used in the war were sprayed from 1965 onward.[19] It is therefore unlikely that effects of dioxin exposure could have been passed from parents to any offspring born before 1965. According to the VAVA criteria, 2,369 Agent Orange victims born between 1965 and 2004 live in Thanh Khe, Cam Le, Hai Chau and Hoa Vang Districts. These are people living with disability; their situation is summarized in the following tables.

Table 2.3. Population, People with Disabilities and Agent Orange Victims with Disabilities in Four Districts of Da Nang

District	Total Population	Total Number of People With Disabilities Aged 5+	Total Number of Agent Orange Victims (AOVs) Aged 5+	AOVs as % of Total PWDs	AOVs as % of Total Population
Thanh Khe	174,557	4,808	451	9.4%	0.3%
Cam Le	87,691	4,735	492	10.4%	0.6%
Hai Chau	189,561	7,232	585	7.4%	0.3%
Hoa Vang	116,524	6,542	891	13.6%	0.8%
Total	568,333	23,317	2,369	10.2%	0.4%

Sources: Vietnam Census 2009, Vietnam Population and Housing Census 2009, VAVA/Da Nang Enumeration 2007

Table 2 shows the number of Agent Orange victims by district and compares their numbers with the total population and the total number of people with disabilities identified in that district by the VPHC.[20] **Agent Orange victims are less than one percent of the population and only about ten percent of all people with disabilities.**

Table 2.4. Agent Orange Victims by Age Group

District	Total Number of AOVs (2007 VAVA Da Nang survey)	Ages			
		Children (5–16 years old)	Youth (17–24 years old)	Adults (25–44 years old)	Adults (45+ years old)
Thanh Khe	451	118	96	237	
Cam Le	492	141	101	250	
Hai Chau	535	139	118	278	
Hoa Vang	891	243	201	447	
Total	2,369	641	516	1,212	
	AOVs in Da Nang	27.1%	21.8%	51.2%	0.0%
	All PWDs in Vietnam	3.2%	3.1%	7.8%	85.8%

Children and youth are the focus of many of the services offered to Agent Orange victims (as well as to other Vietnamese with disabilities). They are slightly less than one half of the Agent Orange victims enumerated in the four districts. The median age is twenty-three. Other Vietnamese with disabilities are overwhelmingly older, as shown in this chart.

Chart 2.1. Agent Orange Victims by Age Group

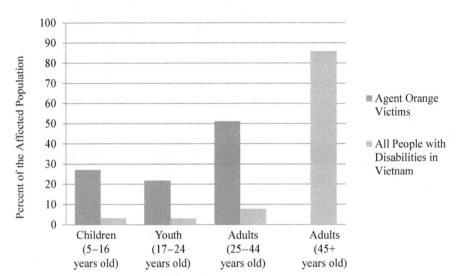

Agent Orange victims as a whole, it can be hypothesized, have lower fertility and higher mortality rates than the general population. The median age would thus increase over time, and the number of Agent Orange victims would diminish. Future services for Agent Orange victims will thus need to shift more and more toward people age twenty-five and older.

Mobility impairments and mental disabilities afflict nearly 90 percent (87.3%) of Agent Orange victims, whereas these kinds of disability affect just under 40 percent of all Vietnamese with disabilities.

Only 12.7% of Agent Orange victims experience impaired hearing, vision and speech, whereas nearly two-thirds of other Vietnamese with disabilities face these challenges. **Future direct services to Agent Orange victims will need to focus primarily on mobility impairments and mental disability.**

Table 2.5. Agent Orange Victims by Type of Disability

District	Number of Respondents	Type of Disability			
		Mobility Impairments	Mental Disabilities	Both Mobility Impairments & Mental Disabilities	Hearing/Vision /Speech Impairments
Thanh Khe	451	189	138	70	54
Cam Le	492	220	114	88	70
Hai Chau	533	202	156	131	44
Hoa Vang	887	384	205	167	131
TOTAL	2,363	995	613	456	299
	AOVs in Da Nang	42.1%	25.9%	19.3%	12.7%
	All PWDs in Vietnam	20.1%	13.6%	5.6%	60.7%

Chart 2.2. Agent Orange Victims by Type of Disability

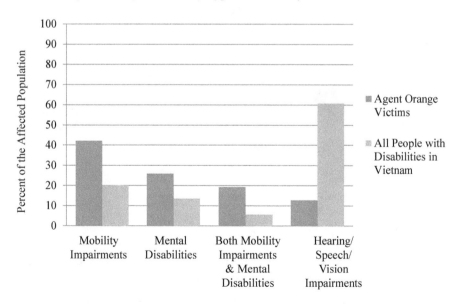

Agent Orange victims also experience disability more severely, as shown in Table 4 and the chart below.

Table 2.6. Agent Orange Victims by Severity of Disability

District	Number of Respondents	Severity		
		Slightly Difficult	Difficult	Very Difficult
Thanh Khe	370	133	149	88
Cam Le	317	124	102	91
Hai Chau	482	219	158	105
Hoa Vang	630	233	272	125
TOTAL	1,799	709	681	409
	AOVs in Da Nang	39.4%	37.9%	22.7%
	All PWDs in Vietnam	60.7%	27.9%	11.4%

Chart 2.3. Agent Orange Victims by Type of Disability

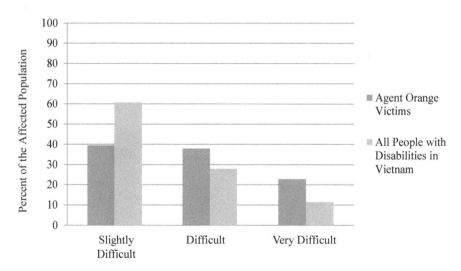

Disability makes life difficult to very difficult, suggesting severe and profound disability, for 60 percent of Agent Orange victims, compared with 40 percent of all Vietnamese with disabilities.

The above data quantify for the first time the situation of a well-defined group of Agent Orange victims in Vietnam. However, a fuller appreciation of what they face comes from the summary descriptions on the dossiers of the 2,369 people in this study. The VAVA teams used the following terms to characterize the disabilities of the Agent Orange victims they identified in Da Nang in 2007.

Physical disabilities: Deformed face, deformed leg, legs or legs and arms; deformed hands, deformed arms and no legs; no legs and missing two fingers; left hand fingers webbed; missing one leg or both legs; missing one arm; missing two arms; no knee joints; weak arms and legs; one leg paralyzed; both legs paralyzed; paralyzed legs and arms; totally paralyzed; leg muscle atrophied; congenital heart disease; cleft palate; narrow chest; crossed arms; inguinal lymph nodes or hernia; restricted growth; skin looks red and bumpy or like snake skin; deaf and mute; spina bifida; visually impaired; difficulties in conversation, mobility.

Mental disabilities: Chronic or congenital mental deficiency; cognitive/ intellectual disability; seizures; schizophrenia; hydrocephalus; Down syndrome; epilepsy; cerebral palsy.

From this discussion we can conclude the following:

- It is not possible to list exactly the actual number of individuals who were exposed to dioxin through the spraying of Agent Orange in Vietnam in the 1960s; the frequency, duration and intensity of their exposure; the resulting levels of dioxin in their bodies or the consequences for their future health and offspring. Nevertheless, one can surmise consequences at the population level in terms of ill health, shortened lives and birth defects.

- It is possible to arrive at credible estimates of the overall prevalence of disabilities among people considered to be Agent Orange victims.

- Although there are potentially new cases arising in the third and fourth generations, Agent Orange victims as a group are aging. They are coping primarily with mobility impairments and mental disabilities rather than hearing, vision or speech impairments. Their disabilities affect them severely.

- The government of Vietnam's criteria for identifying Agent Orange victims are reasonably stringent and should allow programs to address individuals whose conditions are associated with dioxin exposure.

- The overall numbers of people profiled here as Agent Orange victims are large but not beyond the reach of well-funded and efficiently managed programs.

CHAPTER THREE

Does Dioxin Exposure Lead to Birth Defects and Reproductive Failure?

Birth defects are caused by many different factors, and in many cases physicians and medical researchers cannot identify specific causes. Epigenetic studies, however, suggest a relationship between dioxin exposure of a parent and birth defects in their children. Epidemiological studies also point to such a relationship. Three studies from Vietnam established a relationship between exposure during military service and exposure to dioxin "hot spots" and congenital malformations in children. On the other hand, a U.S. Air Force study showed no such relationship for the American servicemen who operated the spray planes. Japanese scientists have demonstrated that dioxin in mothers' milk adversely impacts early childhood development. Further scientific research is needed, but we cannot wait until science provides more conclusive findings to respond.

Birth defects and reproductive failure are the most complicated problems in the discussion of the consequences of Agent Orange in humans, and they are highly controversial. Birth defects are caused by many different factors, and in many cases, physicians and medical researchers cannot identify specific causes. There are many types and degrees of birth defects that place a physical, mental and economic burden on the affected individuals and their families and on society.

The association between parental exposure to Agent Orange or dioxin and birth defects is controversial because of inconsistent findings in the scientific literature. Scientific investigations of the multigenerational health legacy of Agent Orange/dioxin are of three types: environmental/ecological, epigenetic/transgenerational, and epidemiological. The findings of environmental/ecological studies were described in chapter 1. In this chapter we first summarize the epigenetic research and then present a range of findings from epidemiological studies.

Epigenetic Research

Epigenetics is the study of changes that occur in the genome without any alteration in DNA sequence. These changes can switch genes on and off and affect how cells read genes, leading to alterations in gene expression or cellular function. Epigenetic modifications are heritable, can be dynamic, and can be influenced by environmental factors. According to a 2016 article in *Scientific American* that discussed birth defects and Agent Orange, "Scientists are now making important advances that suggest the chemical has long-lasting and even transgenerational effects. Emerging evidence in rodents at labs around the world shows that TCDD alters the epigenome. . . . TCDD can reprogram those epigenetic controls, with consequences that might appear long after the chemical has been cleared from the body."[1] The most recent study (2012) added to earlier findings on rats and "demonstrates that dioxin (TCDD), an environmental toxicant and contaminant present in herbicides such as Agent Orange, can promote epigenetic transgenerational inheritance of diseases in unexposed progeny of the F0 generation females exposed during gestation."[2] Such studies have important implications for risks of environmental exposure to dioxin. In the same *PLOS ONE* article, the authors observe:

The list of diseases seen following exposure of war veterans to Agent Orange (herbicide contaminated with dioxin) during the Vietnam era is growing. Similar observations have been made with the Taiwan, Seveso Italy, China and Japan exposures.

Due to the bioaccumulation of dioxin and up to decade long half-life in humans, any woman becoming pregnant even 20 years after dioxin exposure runs the risk of transmitting dioxin effects to her fetus and later generations. A generational study in the Seveso Italy exposed population supports this concept demonstrating health effects in progeny born 25 years following the exposure. Few studies have addressed this transgenerational aspect of dioxin exposure.

Epidemiological Research

In 2006 a team led by Anh D. Ngo at the University of Texas reviewed thirteen Vietnamese and nine non-Vietnamese studies. They found that "the summary relative risk (RR) of birth defects associated with exposure to Agent Orange was 1.95 (95% confidence interval 1.59–2.39) with substantial heterogeneity across studies. Vietnamese studies showed a higher summary relative risk (RR=3.0; 95% confidence interval 2.19–4.12) than non-Vietnamese studies (RR=1.29; 95% confidence interval level 1.04–1.59). Sub-group analysis found that the magnitude of association tended to increase with greater degrees of exposure to Agent Orange, rated on intensity and duration of exposure and dioxin concentrations measured in affected populations." The authors concluded: "Parental exposure to Agent Orange appears to be associated with an increased risk of birth defects."[3]

In reviewing this study that same year, Arnold Schecter and John D. Constable wrote: "We are of the opinion, based on research beginning even before 1970, that there is no doubt as to the toxicity of the dioxin contaminant of Agent Orange. This dioxin has resulted in serious health effects in humans. We, and many others, have shown elevated levels of TCDD in some Vietnamese, although none of them are now as high as they were in 1970. . . . There is no doubt that during and after the war, many Vietnamese absorbed this very toxic material. It is our belief from toxicological research and epidemiological studies from many countries that this dioxin probably resulted in significant health effects in Vietnam. However, we are not convinced that Vietnamese investigations linking congenital malformations to dioxin are, as yet, more than suggestive. We know of no non-Vietnamese studies linking herbicide or dioxin exposure to congenital malformations other than spina bifida and anencephaly."[4] Whether these non-Vietnamese studies reflect similar levels and duration of exposure to herbicide is unclear. Furthermore, in the study by Anh D. Ngo et al., meta-analysis of only non-Vietnamese publications still revealed a statistically significant link between herbicide exposure and birth defects, though the magnitude of the link is smaller.

Dr. Nguyen Thi Ngoc Phuong was an important early researcher on dioxin exposure and birth defects in Vietnam. During her career she has focused her research on reproductive health, especially in-vitro fertilization. She is the former director of the renowned Tu Du Obstetrics Hospital in Ho Chi Minh City. She testified at the hearings in the United States House of Representatives in 2007 and 2008 on the consequences of herbicides and is a member of the U.S.-Vietnam Dialogue Group on Agent Orange/Dioxin.

Dr. Phuong told us that she has encountered many cases of birth defects at Tu Du Obstetrics Hospital over the course of her career.[5] As early as 1963, newspaper reports on the unusually high incidence of birth defects at Tu Du attracted the attention of the public and some Japanese scientists. From 1965 to 1967, Dr. Phuong collected data on reproductive failure and birth defects in Ben Tre, a province in the Mekong delta where the herbicides were sprayed, and in Ward 10, District 1, Ho Chi Minh City, which had not been sprayed. She found that the rate of birth defects in her survey area in Bien Tre was four or five times the number of birth defects in her survey area in Ho Chi Minh City. In a later study she discovered that women born in 1965 and 1966 had higher rates of reproductive defects and deformed children compared to those born in 1955 and 1956. Normally the reverse would be expected — older women would have higher rates.

She talked with us about the difficulties in the 1970s and 1980s in conducting research on the impact of herbicides on humans in Vietnam. There was not only the lack of money and technology, but also a lack of information and knowledge about the harmful effects of herbicides on the environment and humans in Vietnam. There were many people, including high-ranking leaders, who thought that the mention of the harmful effects of herbicides would affect tourism and the export of agricultural and aquatic products. This fear continued well into the 1990s and even into the early 2000s. To demonstrate the complexity as well as the severe consequences of Agent Orange for generations of children and grandchildren of the people who were exposed, we cite the three principal scientific studies that Vietnamese scientists have conducted over the last three decades. All three studies were carried out by the Military Medical University in Hanoi and compare populations that had a history of Agent Orange exposure with those that did not. Because of the sensitivity of the subject, the study findings were classified and only became available to other Vietnamese and foreign scientists in 2000.

1982 Study — Nguyen Hung Phuc

In 1982, Nguyen Hung Phuc and Cung Binh Trung carried out research on the consequences of toxic chemicals sprayed by the United States on Vietnamese.[6] Subjects of the research were people who were directly sprayed with toxic chemicals in Giong Trom District, Ben Tre Province. A survey of 848 couples showed that 12.20 percent (± 1.44%) suffered miscarriages, an unusually high level. A survey of 3,000 live births before and after spraying in the same area revealed that before the spraying the rate of children born with deformities was 0.14 percent (± 0.08%), and after the spraying the rate was 1.78 percent (± 0.35%).

1999 Study — Nguyen Van Nguyen

From 1996 to 1999 Nguyen Van Nguyen and colleagues conducted a study of birth defects in the areas immediately surrounding the main dioxin hot spots at Bien Hoa, Da Nang and Phu Cat and compared them with a control area, Ha Dong.[7] They surveyed the entire population in each study area. Ha Dong is a rural area in the Red River delta in the north and was never sprayed, although some of its inhabitants may have served in the south and been exposed there during the war. The rate of children born with birth defects per 1,000 people and per 1,000 live births was significantly higher in the areas surrounding the three hot spots than in the control area.

Table 3.1. Rate of Birth Defects

Research Index	Bien Hoa	Da Nang	Phu Cat	Ha Dong
Number of children with birth defects	383	377	296	212
Surveyed population	219,673	172,877	220,895	255,422
Number of live births (accumulated in 22 years)	88,032	70,040	89,425	146,207
Rate of children with birth defects (per 1,000 people)	1.74 ± 0.08	2.18 ± 0.32	1.34 ± 0.21	0.83 ± 0.24
Rate of children with birth defects (per 1,000 live births)	4.35 ± 0.83	5.38 ± 0.79	3.31 ± 0.57	1.45 ± 0.53

2005 Study — Le Bach Quang

In 2005 Le Bach Quang and Doan Huy Hau surveyed 28,817 families of veterans with a history of exposure to Agent Orange and compared them with 19,076 families of veterans with no history of exposure to Agent Orange.[8] Their findings appear in the following table.

Table 3.2. Comparison of Frequency of Veterans' Children with Congenital Malformations

Research Content	Exposed	Not Exposed
Total number of families of veterans	28,817	19,076
Total number of families having children with congenital malformations	1,640	356
Rate of families having children with congenital malformations	5.69%	1.87%
Total number of children with congenital malformations	2,296	452
Total number of live births	77,816	61,043
Rate of children with congenital malformations	2.95%	0.74%

The researchers found a significant difference between the incidence of children born with congenital malformations to veterans who had been exposed to the spraying compared to those who had not.

These studies can be contrasted with the U.S. Air Force Health Study cited in a previous chapter. That investigation compared morbidity, mortality and reproductive health outcomes from 1982 to 2002 for 1,047 servicemen who conducted spraying missions under Operation Ranch Hand with 1,223 Air Force crew and maintenance staff who flew C-130 aircraft elsewhere in Southeast Asia from 1962 to 1971. On reproductive health, the study found that "There was no indication of increased birth defect severity, delays in development, or hyperkinetic syndrome with paternal dioxin. No associations were seen between paternal dioxin level and intrauterine growth retardation."[9]

Researchers led by Teruhiko Kido and Muneko Nishijo at Kanazawa University have carried out studies on dioxin in Vietnam for many years. Kido's research in areas surrounding dioxin hot spots in Bien Hoa and Phu Cat shows that dioxin in breast milk is capable of disrupting the endocrine system in young children.[10] Nishijo's research evaluated the impact of dioxin in mothers' breast milk one month after birth on the physical development of their children. The research showed that body weight and BMI in boys exposed to dioxin through their mother's milk tends to decrease during the four months following birth (Nishijo, 2012) and lasted until the age of 3 (Pham The Tai, 2016). Moreover, early exposure to dioxin can affect neurodevelopment, such as cognitive abilities at four months of age (Pham The Tai, 2013), language skills at one year (Pham The Tai, 2015) and increase the tendency of autism at the age of three (Nishijo, 2014). [11]

In the United States, Elmo R. Zumwalt III, a son of the admiral who ordered the spraying of Agent Orange in Vietnam, and who was exposed to the herbicides himself, died of lymphatic cancer in 1988. Before his death the younger Mr. Zumwalt wrote,

> I am a lawyer and I don't think I could prove in court, by the weight of the existing scientific evidence, that Agent Orange is the cause of all the medical problems — nervous disorders, cancer and skin problems — reported by Vietnam veterans, or of their children's severe birth defects. But I am convinced that it is.[12]

Elmo Zumwalt III's son suffers from severe learning disabilities. His younger brother, James Zumwalt, told us:

> The U.S. government initially did not recognize any correlation between Agent Orange exposure and various cancers and that was the case until the early 1990s. The problem with the Vietnamese government on the other hand was that they asserted that everything — children's birth defects, MS — was all related to AO exposure . . . something wrong was done in Vietnam and we've got to accept responsibility for it. . . . Hopefully the atmosphere now is one that is more conducive to coming up with a joint effort and recognition of what most effectively can be done.[13]

CHAPTER FOUR

Has the Forest Ecology Recovered from the Spraying of Agent Orange?

The spraying of Agent Orange over forests and farmlands defoliated the trees and crops on about 5.5 million acres, destroying the food sources for people and wildlife and eroding and degrading the land. Professor Vo Quy recounts Vietnam's early attempts to assess the damage. Few data exist on these complex ecosystems prior to the spraying, and this prevents putting an economic value on the loss. The coastal mangrove swamps recovered only to be cut back later with the expansion of shrimp cultivation. The ecological complexity of the former upland forests has been replaced with plantations of single species forests or remains barren land. Pilot projects have demonstrated how to reforest degraded lands in a way that creates new economic opportunities for rural people, restores biodiversity and re-establishes ecological balance.

T he spraying of Agent Orange by the United States left behind nearly 5 million acres of denuded or heavily defoliated upland and coastal forests in southern Vietnam – about 36 percent of the total mangrove forest area – and damaged some 500,000 acres of rice and other crops.[1] The total impacted area was nearly the size of the American state of Massachusetts. In the decades since the spraying stopped, many of the coastal mangrove forests revived only to be cut back as Vietnamese farmers began to intensively farm shrimp and black tiger prawns for export. Since the 1990s Vietnam has also worked to re-habilitate and reforest large areas of bare hills in the uplands with fast-growing mono-crops of eucalyptus and acacia species. Nevertheless, decades after the end of the spraying of Agent Orange, many upland ecosystems have not yet recovered. It would take centuries, at least, to fully reproduce the ecologically balanced mix of flora and fauna that once thrived there.

Well before the end of the war, the government of Vietnam began to assess the impacts of the herbicides on the environment in the then-South Vietnam. They selected a young ornithologist, Vo Quy, to lead a reconnaissance mission into the war-torn south in 1971 and again in 1974. Professor Quy recounted his experiences in his memoir:

> I still remember clearly, in early 1971, Professor Ton That Tung . . . told me "The issue of toxic chemicals in South Vietnam is immense but I can just do research into its effects on people. It would be great if you can research its impact on animals and the environment."
>
> At that time the war of the Vietnamese people against the Americans was very fierce in South Vietnam while North Viet-nam suffered daily bombardment and shelling from the American military. Although there was very little information available, I had heard that the U.S. military had sprayed herbicides to defoli-ate large areas of forest in provinces in the South, but, according to them, it does not kill the trees. However, the news from South Vietnam was that the spraying caused not just mass death of forest trees, but also of forest animals and domestic livestock. As a biolo-gist, I wanted to learn more about the toxic chemical that the U.S. had sprayed in South Vietnam. Thus I accepted Prof. Tung's offer to participate in the research.
>
> The only way to do research on the consequences of the U.S. chemical warfare on the environment and on biological species was to go to the battlefield and conduct on-the-spot surveys of places where the U.S. had sprayed the toxic chemical. In 1971, I was selected to join a group of seven scientific officers from dif-ferent state agencies who voluntarily headed to South Vietnam to do research on the U.S. herbicides. We were allowed to accompany the army troops who were moving from the North to the South. Although our group was scientific officers, we were equipped with

guns and ammunition so we could be ready to fight if we had to face the enemy. Over a hard week, we reached Vinh Linh District, located to the north of the 17th parallel. . . . We waited here a couple of days, living in historic Vinh Moc tunnel, unable to find a way to cross the Ben Hai River and head further to the South. Finally, we decided to stay in Vinh Linh for the research.

The research site was Ru Lenh area, which used to be a small forbidden forest before the war. It was about 10 square kilometers in extent and located to the north of the Ben Hai River but the area had been sprayed with herbicides by the U.S. military. Although the area was small, it was the first time I had seen firsthand the devastation of the defoliants that the U.S. used. The entire forest including plenty of big trees had died, and had been chopped to pieces by bombs and bullets, not just having been defoliated as the U.S. side had declared. The residents living here said that all fish, chicken, and ducks also died of the poison and there had even been cases of dogs born with deformities. Because of having too many difficulties, our team had to sadly return after more than a week working in Vinh Linh. Although the research period was too short, we had an overview of the harmful effects of the toxic chemical on nature and this made us determined to continue doing research on it.

In early 1974, I was allowed to go to the South to do research on the toxic chemicals for the second time. . . . To perform the assigned tasks, I selected nine officers, mostly lecturers from Hanoi National University[2]. . . . All participated voluntarily despite potential life threatening dangers. The team departed from Hanoi in early February 1974, heading along the Truong Son route and following the guidance of the military stations to ensure safety. This journey was full of difficulties, but much easier than the first one, with less bombardment and shelling. Occasionally, we saw reconnaissance aircraft flying overhead. . . .

At the battlefields and in the places that had been sprayed with herbicides, not having other tools, I used my binoculars to identify each bird species that appeared and to see if their nests were new or old, then carefully recorded this information in my notebook. At that time, animals in the sprayed forest areas were scarcely seen. In a large forest dozens of square kilometers in extent, only dead and dried trees of various sizes were seen; there were places that had been burned black by napalm bombs; and the forest was totally deserted, without a bird singing, an ape howling, nor a frog or a bee appearing nor the cries of insects. There were no green trees, food, and shelter left for them. The scene was extremely horrific. Coming here, standing between hundreds of thousands of dead trees, and seeing all a grey color, one could really feel how an exterminated ecosystem looked like, or what an 'ecocide' was, as Prof. Arthur Galston of Yale University in the United States, once condemned the U.S. chemical warfare in Vietnam.

In fierce battlefields where death was so close, many soldiers were astonished at why there were people coming here just to find birds or their nests. However, it was birds that helped me understand the severity of the consequences that the toxic chemical had caused to each region. I used my knowledge about bird species as a tool for research. I used birds as an environmental indicator. The absence of bird species let me know the extent of the toxic chemical contamination in the research areas. *'Birds perch on the sound land'* (a Vietnamese saying).

The mangrove forest . . . once had diverse species of birds, mostly water birds. After having been sprayed with herbicide, the birds disappeared. They died due to direct exposure to dioxin or eating dioxin-contaminated shrimp or fish. Dioxin accumulated in the bodies of the birds and in their eggs, thus, the eggs when laid were unable to hatch. Shortly after that, the birds gradually disappeared. Currently, however, bird species have returned in some regions, with increasing numbers, as in places we were conducting the survey. Some birds have come back and nested densely. This means bird food such as shrimps, and small fishes in some mangrove forest areas is no longer dioxin-contaminated, and water environment and surface mud do not contain dioxin residue.

In more than three months in the battlefields in the South, our team visited different sprayed regions along the Truong Son route to Quang Tri, Thua Thien-Hue, Kon Tum, Gia Lai, and Dac Lac Provinces. . . . Seeing for myself the devastated forests everywhere, the idea of environmental research became clearer in my mind. I thought about restoring the forests and their biological species after the war and helping local residents reuse the lands ravaged by the war. I have pursued and sought ways to try making these ideas come true. Till now, I understand that it is a difficult work, requiring a lot of effort and resources. The knowledge of the toxic chemical gained from this survey and others in later years has been very useful to me when I was asked to join the U.S.-Vietnam Dialogue Groups on Agent Orange/dioxin in 2007.[3]

The 10-80 Committee and later the Office of Committee 33 sponsored several research projects to evaluate the loss of biodiversity in the Truong Son Mountains and adverse biological changes to the environment in the heavily dioxin-contaminated areas. The most recent of these projects has sought to evaluate the overall environmental damages caused by herbicides by focusing on several questions:

- How much forest area was destroyed?
- How many cubic meters of wood were lost?
- What is the extent of the biodiversity degradation?
- What is the value of the species of plants and animals that have disappeared?
- How should one calculate the value of land that is degraded and no longer suited for cultivation?
- What is the impact on ground and surface water?
- How can the environment be restored and how much will this cost?[4]

However, the scientists concluded it was not possible to estimate the environmental losses at such a level of detail and for every component of the environment. The great complexity of the environment and the lack of sufficient data about complex subtropical ecosystems in past decades prevent a comprehensive assessment. We can, however, state several conclusions and point to some remedies.

Soil erosion and landslides have sharply reduced soil nutrients and altered runoff patterns. Invasive grasses of low value have taken hold in many areas. The loss of trees, biological diversity and usable cropland has slowed development and led to economic stagnation, poverty and malnutrition. Animal and bird species have suffered from habitat loss; some are now in danger of extinction.[5]

The most heavily sprayed areas were in the Rung Sat Special Zone, along the rivers approaching Saigon, the Ca Mau peninsula south of the Mekong Delta, and the upland forests of Ma Da, Phu Binh, Sa Thay and Aluoi. Some areas were sprayed more than four times; 34 percent of the regions were sprayed more than once. Areas along the Laos and Cambodia borders were also sprayed. The total area covered included about 15 percent of southern Vietnam.[6]

Has the landscape recovered? Only in part. The most severe defoliation was in coastal mangrove forests, where extensive stands of the dominant tree (*Rhizophora apiculata*) were killed. Shrubs below were heavily defoliated but generally survived. Areas around the 17th parallel, near the former demilitarized zone (DMZ) near the Laotian border, remain denuded. Most of the triple-canopy forests were replaced by invasive weeds (villagers call some varieties "American grass"), tussock grass and bamboo. Regeneration has been slow because of degraded soils, hillside erosion and repeated flooding and fires. Intensive mangrove replanting has occurred in some areas.

What was the impact on area residents? Villagers harvested the dead mangroves for fuel, but many who had depended upon forest crops and hunting lost their livelihoods. In areas where crops were destroyed, barren soils became heavily eroded, losing fertility, and many farmers abandoned their lands. They suffered unemployment, poverty and malnutrition as a result.

Is reforestation possible? Yes, and necessary, because natural regrowth could take more than a century, with unpredictable results. Active replanting with ecologically viable trees and shrubs with economic value would require substantial and sustained long-term investment.[7] The Vietnamese have already demonstrated the promise of several interventions. These are some examples.

In the 1970s the government began a program to replant ravaged coastal mangrove forests with seedlings of *Rhizophora apicauda*. Some 70,000 hectares (173,000 acres) of forest have been replanted and are now a self-sustaining and profitable source of fuel and wood for construction.

Southeast of Ho Chi Minh City, in the Can Gio District, more than 85,000 acres of mangroves were nearly destroyed. Now, 55,000 acres have been replanted and are thriving well enough to be included in the Biospheres World Network of Unesco's Man and Biosphere Program.[8]

In 2008 Professor Vo Quy and the Center for Natural Resources and Environmental Studies launched a project in central Quang Tri Province that trained ninety-one farmers and ninety-two farm managers and technicians in habitat restoration and damaged land re-use techniques. Residents of other regions have requested similar courses. In the Ma Da Forest, trainers demonstrated the use of a cover crop of fast-growing acacia trees, which after three years are tall enough to shade forest tree seedlings from the intense tropical sun. Farmers then plant seedlings of indigenous tree species, such as dipterocarps, beneath the acacia.[9]

In Aloui District, in the mountains west of Hue 256, spraying missions denuded 175,000 acres around three former U.S. Special Forces bases. Phung Tuu Boi of the Center for Assistance in Nature Conservation and Community Development initiated a project to plant "green fences" of honey locust trees with long thorns (*Gleditschia australis*) around the worst-contaminated areas of the former A So Air Base to prevent further human and animal exposure. The trees thrive on rocky soils, are resistant to insects and diseases and live 50 to 60 years. In four to five years, the fruit from the trees can be used or sold to produce soaps, shampoo and medicines, covering the costs of maintaining the trees and providing a source of household income.

In 1998 the Hue University of Agriculture and Forestry began research on smallholder agriculture in the uplands and used the findings to train farmers to take advantage of new technologies and marketing opportunities. Under the direction of Dr. Le Van An, the university now operates a farm extension center in Aluoi District that introduces farmers to new techniques and opportunities in agroforestry.

These and similar initiatives are starting points to reforest degraded areas in a way that re-establishes ecological balance, preserves and restores biodiversity, helps combat global warming and improves the lives of local people.

CHAPTER FIVE

What Do Americans Know About Agent Orange, and How Are They Prepared to Help?

In 2009 a public opinion polling firm in the United States surveyed Americans on what they knew about Agent Orange in Vietnam and whether they wanted to see their government assist Vietnamese impacted by it. The poll found that many Americans are aware of Agent Orange but not that it continues to impact Vietnam today. The key to gaining their support is to overcome this lack of awareness and frame the issue as an humanitarian effort that will help the people of Vietnam solve a problem that has gone on far too long. This study continues to be the best guide to target audiences and effective messages for reaching Americans about Agent Orange.

In thinking about the United States, Vietnamese commonly distinguish between the U.S. government and the American people. While the U.S. government has been hostile to Vietnam, the American people themselves understand, sympathize and support the Vietnamese. Does this dichotomy apply to the issue of Agent Orange? What do Americans today know about Agent Orange in Vietnam? Do they want to see the United States actively assist the Vietnamese impacted by Agent Orange? And are they ready to press their government to do so?

To examine these questions, in 2009 the Agent Orange in Vietnam Information Initiative (AOVII)[1] commissioned Belden Russonello & Stewart (now Belden Russonello Strategists—BRS), a Washington-based communications research firm, to conduct six focus groups on Agent Orange across the United States, followed by a national survey of registered voters. The BRS work reported here was the first, and so far the only, national survey of registered voters in the United States on the subject of Agent Orange in Vietnam. Registered voters are more likely than the American public at large to be informed and engaged with issues of the day and to vote and otherwise make their views known to public officials. They are the relevant group for efforts to influence public policy through the mass media.

Two conclusions emerged from the survey:

- First, the knowledge, beliefs and attitudes of registered voters about Agent Orange and Vietnam were diverse and not simple. Voters did not necessarily understand, sympathize or support the Vietnamese position. A general informational media campaign across the United States could therefore be counterproductive. Leadership from the United States Congress would be particularly important.

- Second, the attitudes of the registered voters accurately predicted the form that American assistance to Vietnam for Agent Orange would later take — support to clean up the major dioxin hot spots and assistance at the level of tens of millions of dollars per year channeled through nongovernmental organizations to help Vietnamese with disabilities.[2]

The Focus Groups

Because BRS believed veterans could play a key role — either in favor or opposed to action — the firm conducted one of the focus groups among American veterans of Vietnam and another among people under thirty-five who had served in the military. The participants in the other four groups were chosen to represent audiences that BRS believed might have an interest in the topic of Agent Orange and dioxin in Vietnam. Two groups comprised environmental-leaning men and women — one group of people in their fifties and sixties (known in the United States as baby boomers) and one group of people in their twenties and thirties. The fifth focus group contained baby boomers who put a high priority on peace and improving American relations with foreign countries.

The final group included men and women in their twenties and thirties who support American efforts to address the health needs of people in other countries. All the participants were voters and active participants in their communities across the United States.

From the focus groups, BRS identified two key challenges for an outreach effort: First, overcome the lack of awareness among Americans of the lingering effects of Agent Orange on the people of Vietnam; and second, appeal to the value of responsibility in a positive, nonthreatening manner. American assistance should be framed as a contribution to an international humanitarian effort that will help the people of Vietnam solve a problem that has gone on for too long. BRS noted, "The focus groups sent us a very clear message that the primary motive for helping is collective guilt — as long as the guilt is not applied directly."[3]

These conclusions emerged from the focus groups.

- A personal connection with the Vietnam War produced strong feelings in many of the people in the focus groups. The group of Vietnam veterans showed the most awareness of Agent Orange and its impacts, and some of them were among the most likely to support action to remedy the situation. The baby boomers who actively opposed the war, or at least lived through it, were also more likely to have strong feelings than the younger voters in the groups who have little connection with the war. BRS reported, "The more involved an individual was in Vietnam, the more he or she feels responsible for the devastation."[4]

- Responsibility was the main value underlying the attitudes of the participants in the focus groups. Some felt what they described as a "moral responsibility" for the United States to repair the damage it caused during the war as soon as they heard about its ongoing impacts. Others resisted U.S. efforts to help because "bad things happen during a war" and they did not want to take responsibility for what happened nearly 50 years ago. Still others struggled to decide what responsibility Americans owe to the Vietnamese people.

- Outreach messaging should highlight responsibility, but gently. The focus group members who were most likely to commit to helping win support for American assistance to Vietnam were comfortable with hearing a message directly about America's responsibility. For others, highlighting that innocent people are still being harmed by a conflict that happened before they were born makes the human cost of the tragedy clear without pointing a finger of blame.

- Asking the United States to join with charitable organizations, the country of Vietnam and other countries in an effort to clean up the dioxin and treat its effects "soothes the fears of those who are worried about the U.S. acknowledging fault for its behavior in Vietnam. . . . They see U.S. responsibility more positively, as doing the right thing and playing its role as world leader, rather than as making up for past sins."[5]

- Except for a few of the baby boomers and Vietnam veterans, it had never occurred to most participants that Agent Orange might still be affecting people in Vietnam, even if they knew that U.S. veterans have fought to have the government recognize its impacts on servicemen and women. They need to hear that Vietnam continues to struggle with the effects of those chemicals. Most are completely unfamiliar with the chemical dioxin, so starting communications with "Agent Orange" will be clearer for these voters.

- The key to gaining support is to indicate this is a problem Americans know how to solve. Without a solution, many of the participants started to tune out. The easiest way to approach a solution is to assert that the United States should start by cleaning up the dioxin hot spots. Hot-spot cleanup is the most approachable part of the solution because it is most easily understood and because voters believe that it will stop the human suffering from continuing. BRS reported that participants said that "efforts to help the suffering of people already afflicted should be a secondary priority, both because they see this kind of effort as more difficult and expensive, and also because they say without cleaning up the hot spots, we will just have to help the next generation and the next."[6]

- Channeling American assistance through NGOs makes the effort feel safer and more likely to succeed. Participants felt it was important for nonprofits to handle the money rather than having it go directly to the government of Vietnam. They also worried that advocates would demand billions of dollars for this issue, which could detract from other things they cared about. Informing them that the effort is in the millions of dollars makes it seem more doable, and stretching a total amount out over a decade rather than all at once was easier for many to accept.

- The greatest barriers to progress on the Agent Orange issue are lack of knowledge about it and some participants' feelings that there are more pressing issues in the United States that demand time and resources.

The National Survey

BRS used these findings to design and carry out a nationally representative survey[7] of registered voters on their attitudes toward American aid to Vietnam to help address the impacts of Agent Orange. The survey was conducted through 1,200 telephone interviews using both landlines and cellphones from November 3 to 17, 2009. BRS then weighted the data by gender, race, age and education to bring them into proper proportions with registered voters in the country as a whole. The margin of sampling error was plus or minus 2.8 percentage points.

Key Findings

Many Americans are aware of Agent Orange but not of its lingering impacts on Vietnam.

More than three-quarters of registered voters in the survey say they have heard of Agent Orange (77 percent) while only 23 percent say they have not. Most of them can offer a definition that shows they have some sense of what it was (67 percent).

Another large majority of voters, when reminded how Agent Orange was used during the war, says that it had harmful effects on people's health (76 percent). A smaller majority (54 percent) is convinced that U.S. veterans who were exposed to it are still suffering the ill effects. However, only three in ten believe that people in Vietnam are still affected (31 percent).

Chart 5.1. Registered U.S. Voters' Knowledge of the Impact of Agent Orange

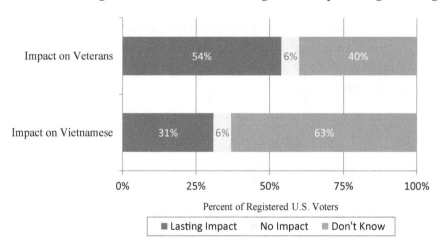

Politics and education are the best predictors of Americans who are the most likely to support assistance to Vietnam on Agent Orange.

Statistical analysis of the data showed that the three demographic factors that best predict support for aid to Vietnam are ideology (liberals), political party (Democrats) and education (higher). That is, Democrats, liberals and those with higher levels of education are more likely to be supportive. Because voters under age thirty are more likely to be liberal and Democratic, they are also more likely to be supportive. Voters over fifty, who tend to be more conservative, are less supportive. Americans were more or less evenly divided on aid to Vietnam in 2009: 54 percent opposed assistance and 47 percent were in favor of it.

Chart 5.2. Support for U.S. Help in Vietnam Generally

	Strongly Oppose	Somewhat Oppose	Strongly Support	Somewhat Support
Total	21%	33%	17%	23%
18-29	16%	24%	28%	24%
30-39	27%	29%	20%	20%
40-49	23%	36%	11%	25%
50-59	19%	34%	17%	22%
60+	19%	37%	12%	26%
≤High School	21%	36%	15%	23%
Some College	24%	33%	16%	21%
College Graduate	21%	28%	17%	26%
Post-Graduate	15%	24%	29%	24%
Liberal	17%	23%	26%	26%
Moderate	20%	32%	15%	28%
Conservative	22%	38%	14%	20%

Other factors that the researchers thought might play a role turned out to make little difference. For example, having opposed the war in Vietnam in the 1960s and '70s does not make a person more likely to support helping the country of Vietnam today. Their support for action is little more than that of Americans as a whole. This is not surprising, given that the survey analysis reveals that Americans support aid because of current humanitarian concerns, not historical references to the war.

Information about the impacts of Agent Orange generates concern among Americans.

When presented with information, a majority of voters expressed high levels of concern about three specific pieces of information:

- The Vietnamese Red Cross reports that 3 million people in Vietnam have been affected by Agent Orange/dioxin (51 percent very concerned).

- During the war in Vietnam, the American military sprayed Agent Orange at up to fifty times the concentration recommended by manufacturers (55 percent).

- The United States Department of Veterans Affairs acknowledges that Agent Orange has played a major role in many diseases and assists veterans who served in Vietnam and now suffer from these diseases (62 percent).

Chart 5.3. Concern about Agent Orange

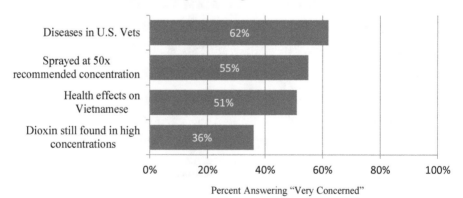

Percent Answering "Very Concerned"

Several elements of proposals to assist Vietnam are popular:

- Three-quarters of voters (76 percent) favor "supporting education and job training for people with disabilities caused by Agent Orange so they can improve their quality of life" (45 percent strongly support, 31 percent somewhat support).

- Three-quarters (75 percent) also support "funding programs that provide medical care and rehabilitation services for people with illnesses and disabilities caused by Agent Orange" (43 percent strongly, 32 percent somewhat).

- A similar number (73 percent) support "cleaning up the toxic hot spots caused by Agent Orange and dioxin so that future generations are not exposed to these dangerous chemicals" (44 percent strongly, 29 percent somewhat).

- More than seven of every ten voters surveyed (73 percent) favor "supporting research on the effects Agent Orange has had on human health and the environment" (39 percent strongly, 34 percent somewhat).

- Two-thirds (66 percent) favor "supporting reforestation projects that will restore the ecosystem that was damaged by Agent Orange" (33 percent strongly, 33 percent somewhat).

Statistical analysis shows that strong support for cleaning up toxic hot spots also strongly predicts support for the program of assistance as a whole.

The following groups are more likely to favor all of the above proposals: women, younger voters, African-Americans, Hispanics, Democrats, liberals, non-Christians, those who opposed the Vietnam War and supporters of foreign aid in general. Veterans are less likely to favor them.

Rationales in favor of helping Vietnam are not compelling.

Voters overall do not strongly support any of the reasons the BRS survey offered for the United States to help Vietnam. No more than two out of ten voters said that any of the following rationales for action is "extremely convincing" on a 10-point scale.

Chart 5.4. Rationales for U.S. Contribution Efforts

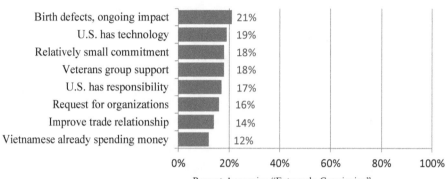

Percent Answering "Extremely Convincing"

For some of the reasons, those who said the reason to help was "not convincing at all" outnumbered those who found it "very convincing." This was particularly true for the claim of U.S. responsibility (27 percent found it not at all a convincing reason), the information that the Vietnamese government is already contributing (22 percent not at all convincing) and the idea of encouraging a good trade relationship (22 percent not at all convincing).

The needs of American veterans and other priorities at home hold strong counterappeal.

On the opposition side, many voters responded to the idea that the U.S. government should help its own veterans before helping Vietnam (50 percent "extremely convincing") and/or expressed concerns that there are too many needs of the moment at home for the United States to be helping other countries (33 percent). Less convincing rationales against aid included criticisms of the Vietnamese government, that the United States does not have a responsibility to help or that Agent Orange has not been proved scientifically to be the cause of problems.

Chart 5.5. Reasons Not to Support U.S. Help in Vietnam

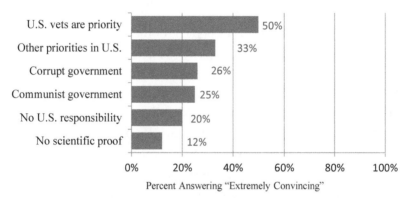

The BRS survey analysis concluded that a media outreach campaign should be targeted rather than general because a general appeal would result in awakening more opponents than supporters of aid to Vietnam. "The price of trying to reach beyond the strong supporters — to win over those in the middle — will be to arouse the potentially strong opponents of aid to Vietnam. . . . Concentrated activism from a few on a relatively low-profile issue such as this could prove decisive."[8]

The Agent Orange in Vietnam Information Initiative consolidated the BRS findings into a three-minute animated video, "Make Agent Orange History." The video conveys the messages and values most likely to move Americans to action, and it continues to be popular on YouTube (https://www.youtube.com/watch?v=Zx1f9hebiGg).

In the years since the BRS survey, United States-Vietnam relations have improved and deepened across the board, including cooperation to address war legacies. Congress has appropriated funds for aid to Vietnam on Agent Orange year after year, and there is much less reason today for the concern that BRS identified in 2009. The need to inform Americans about Agent Orange continues, and efforts to do so can certainly aim to reach everyone in America. A communications strategy for Agent Orange, however, necessarily must focus its resources on messages that resonate with key groups of Americans and motivate them to take action. The BRS study findings continue to be the best, and only, guide to key audiences and effective messages. It singled out four groups in particular.

Young voters

Voters under thirty made up 18 percent of the total population of registered voters. In this group a majority (52 percent) supported a generous annual allocation of aid to Vietnam, more than any other age group. Young voters were also more likely to respond to messages in favor of action and to embody characteristics that predict action, including being more liberal and more Democratic. Young voters are more likely to be getting their news online (33 percent) than from any other source, and are less likely than most to be watching cable television (32 percent) or reading a print newspaper (5 percent). Three-quarters (73 percent) are using social networking websites, and nearly half are using social networking to communicate about social causes or organizations. These trends have surely intensified since the survey was taken.

Supporters over fifty

These were voters who were over fifty years of age and who somewhat or strongly supported aid to Vietnam after hearing information and messages about Agent Orange. They made up 17 percent of the whole population of registered voters, and 39 percent of registered voters over fifty. Older supporters are more likely than the population as a whole to read a newspaper in print (21 percent), although like everyone else they are most likely to get their news from cable TV (36 percent). They are much less likely to be getting their news online (9 percent).

Veteran supporters

This target audience comprised those who have served in the armed forces of the United States and who support aid to Vietnam after hearing information and messages. They make up 6 percent of the population of registered voters. Twenty-nine percent of veteran supporters describe themselves as Vietnam veterans. Like the public as a whole, veteran supporters were divided on the war in Vietnam as it was happening (20 percent supported it, 17 percent opposed, 12 percent were neutral and the rest are too young to have had an opinion at the time). Veteran supporters are more likely than the population as a whole to be listening to National Public Radio, or NPR, (12 percent) and less likely to be watching cable television (25 percent).

Those who opposed the war in Vietnam

This group consisted of voters who were over fifty-five and said they opposed the war in Vietnam at the time it was happening. These voters made up 11 percent of the electorate. After hearing information and messages about aid to Vietnam, 46 percent of those who opposed the Vietnam War at the time favored a current program of aid to help Vietnam recover from Agent Orange. A quarter (26 percent) said that a message about U.S. responsibility for damage caused in Vietnam is not at all convincing, while about the same number (24 percent) say it is extremely convincing. People in this group were more likely to be reading a newspaper (22 percent) than was the general population, and they got most of their news from cable television (33 percent). Online news was not popular among this group (7 percent).

These groups are a good focus and starting point for any future efforts to reach the American public through the mass media with messages about Agent Orange in Vietnam.

Communications should lead with a description of the current problems in Vietnam. It is not safe to assume that even those who are most supportive of helping Vietnam are aware that Agent Orange and dioxin continue to affect Vietnamese people today. In some cases, they may not even be certain about the meaning of the term Agent Orange. Communications should start by asserting that Agent Orange is still a problem in Vietnam and giving some data to back up that assertion. Supporters of aid to Vietnam become even more enthusiastic about their support when they know about specific projects and what they are accomplishing. The completion of cleanup at Phu Cat, the progress at Da Nang and the plans to clean up Bien Hoa are exciting because they show that it is possible to stop the problem from continuing to affect future generations. This excitement then makes it easier to draw attention to the Agent Orange victims and their needs and build support for projects of meaningful assistance.

Finally, one of the strongest correlations to support for helping Vietnam is support for humanitarian aid in general. The messages that gain the most traction are humanitarian as well: they focus on the human costs of Agent Orange in terms of children suffering from birth defects and disabilities, and an assertion that the United States can make a great deal of difference at little cost.

CHAPTER SIX

What Is Vietnam Doing for the Victims of Agent Orange?

In the current economic and social conditions of Vietnam, a majority of families with disabled members, including Agent Orange victims, face many challenges. Vietnam assists Agent Orange victims through a system of social supports that continues to be developed and expanded. In 2016 there were 335,558 Agent Orange victims receiving government assistance under a 2012 ordinance, and 465,000 Agent Orange victims were receiving help through charitable donations from the public.

A gent Orange victims in Vietnam have different characteristics compared to Agent Orange victims among American veterans and veterans in the allied countries who fought in the war in Vietnam.

First, they have more time of exposure to Agent Orange with greater exposure intensity, and it is more likely that Agent Orange enters their body through contact with contaminated soils and the digestive tract because they have lived for a long time in the sprayed areas. Second, the nutrition and medical care available in Vietnam during the years of war and even decades after the war were poor and rudimentary. Many victims died of the diseases that had not been detected or could not be treated properly.

Thus, the patterns and characteristics of diseases of the victims in Vietnam are more diverse and more serious. Disease is one of the main things that make the economic and cultural life, education and vocational training of the victims and their descendants difficult and create a vicious cycle in their lives.

In the economic and social conditions of Vietnam, a country that has endured many wars and until recent times was an overwhelmingly rural and impoverished country, a majority of families with disabled people, of whom many are Agent Orange victims, meet many difficulties. They need health care and improvement of their material and spiritual life. In particular, we need to pay attention to the mental burden that they and their families have suffered.

The Vietnamese Government has had many positive activities to research and overcome the consequences of Agent Orange immediately after the war ended. In October 1980, the Vietnamese Government established the Committee for Investigating the Consequences of Toxic Chemicals Used by the U.S. in the War in Vietnam (also known as the 10-80 Committee). It was placed in the Ministry of Health. In addition to researching and investigating the consequences of Agent Orange, the committee also mobilized foreign nongovernmental organizations to build a system of Peace Villages to care for children with birth defects.

In March 1999, to step up the organization of activities surrounding the Agent Orange legacy, the Vietnamese government established the National Steering Committee for Overcoming the Consequences of Toxic Chemicals Used by the U.S. in the War in Vietnam (Committee 33). Committee 33 has been implementing both research and efforts to measure and remediate the residual dioxin at former U.S. military bases. In 1999, the Vietnam Red Cross established the National Fund for Victims of Agent Orange in Vietnam, which has been replicated by Red Cross Societies in provinces and cities.

The Vietnam Association of Victims of Agent Orange (VAVA) came into being in 2004. Its main task is to raise funds and assist Agent Orange victims. Like the Red Cross, there are VAVA branches now in most provinces, cities and districts. With this system of organizations, networks for assisting the victims of Agent Orange have been established across the country.

There are some children's feeding centers under the Ministry of Labor, Invalids and Social Affairs, as well as the Red Cross Society and the Veterans Association. These facilities are still small and lack equipment and funds for operation, so they are unable to assist all children with birth defects. Most children with birth defects are cared for at home, so they receive little rehabilitation and necessary skills training.

On June 17, 2010, the National Assembly approved the Law on Disabled People, which states the rights of Vietnamese with disabilities and the responsibilities of the government to provide services to them in their communities, including rehabilitation centers, job training and placement, and monthly stipends for the most severely disabled.

Two years later, on July 16, 2012, the Standing Committee of the National Assembly revised the ordinance for people with meritorious services to the revolution to include services and benefits for those considered to be victims of toxic chemicals.[1] Under Article 26 of this ordinance, a monthly allowance is given to those who worked, fought and provided services in the sprayed areas during the resistance war from August 1961 to April 30, 1975, and who were exposed to toxic chemicals and later experienced a reduction in the capacity to work by 21 percent or more, infertility or birth defects in their offspring. Article 27 authorizes health insurance and prosthetic devices according to need and availability of state funds. Beneficiaries can visit a sanatorium every two years. Those whose work capacity has been reduced by 81 percent or more can visit a sanatorium every year, receive a monthly allowance for household help and enjoy tax exemption.

In 2014 there were 286,093 Agent Orange victims receiving benefits under the 2012 ordinance, and their monthly allowances totaled 4.7 trillion Vietnamese dong (VND) for the year, equivalent to $230 million at the time.[2] By the end of 2016, the number of Agent Orange victims who were receiving benefits under the 2012 ordinance had grown to 335,558.[3] The 2012 ordinance applies only to resistance war activists suffering diseases and/or having children with congenital deformities due to exposure to Agent Orange. Other Agent Orange victims, those who were not resistance activists or who served in the Saigon army or government and their offspring, receive support through charitable donations to local social welfare organizations or branches of the Vietnam Association of Victims of Agent Orange. In 2016, some 465,000 Agent Orange victims were receiving help from these sources. This assistance is still small and unpredictable and does not ensure high efficiency and sustainability.[4]

CHAPTER SEVEN

What Has the United States Done So Far?

Between 1989 and 2007, USAID drew on the Leahy War Victims Fund for projects assisting disabled Vietnamese who had come in contact with unexploded ordnance. In 2007, the U.S. Congress began appropriating funds to address a second war legacy in Vietnam, Agent Orange/dioxin. Over time the appropriations have grown, supporting projects for people with disabilities without regard to cause and cleanup of dioxin-contaminated soils at former American military bases. Official American assistance since 2007 totals $231.2 million (including $30.0 million anticipated in FY 2018). Eighty percent of the funds have been for cleanup and 20 percent for services, primarily in Da Nang. Private American assistance has totaled $31.1 million These actions have shown the goodwill of the U.S. government in addressing the consequences of Agent Orange in Vietnam.

Until 2007, the officials of the two governments held quite different perspectives and took different approaches when they talked to each other about Agent Orange. From the U.S. perspective, the State Department was seeking to build a new relationship with Vietnam oriented to the future, and discussions of Agent Orange only served to reopen the past. There were also concerns that assistance to Vietnam could potentially become large and open-ended as well as set a precedent for environmental cleanup elsewhere.

But in 2007 things began to change. Other themes and topics within the bilateral relationship had begun to blossom and deepen. The government of Vietnam appointed Dr. Le Ke Son, a medical doctor and toxicologist, to lead discussions with the United States. On the American side, Ambassador Michael W. Marine told Dr. Charles Bailey that he felt that the United States had a moral responsibility to address the Agent Orange legacy.

Two other American actors then entered the scene and pushed the issue forward.

The Ford Foundation mobilized other American foundations, businesses, the United Nations and some foreign governments to provide the early funds, or seed money, to kick-start joint cooperative work on environmental cleanup and help to Agent Orange victims. These actions from mainstream American organizations encouraged the U.S. Congress to channel larger sums of money to the executive branch and require it to use them in Vietnam for Agent Orange.

The same year, the Senate Appropriations Committee of the Congress took up the Agent Orange legacy issue and approved an initial amount of $3 million for the United States to begin to tackle it. Senator Patrick Leahy led this initiative; as he would later put it, "I recall vividly when Vietnamese officials, who expressed appreciation for our support for UXO programs and other areas of cooperation, would bring up Agent Orange. The whole tenor of the conversation would change. They would insist that the United States should take care of the victims of Agent Orange, whom they numbered in the millions, and clean up the areas that were contaminated with dioxin."

Senator Leahy's reference to UXO programs concerned efforts to reduce harm from unexploded ordnance (UXO), or shells and bombs left behind by the Americans that were still harming Vietnamese. "They always brought it [Agent Orange] up, and they were not shy about expressing their anger about it," said Mr. Leahy, a Democrat and the senior senator from Vermont. He went on to say:

> Frankly, it was hard to argue with them. If Agent Orange contaminated with dioxin were sprayed today over inhabited areas and rice

fields as it was in Vietnam back then, it would likely be considered a war crime. I felt that instead of turning our backs on the problem we had a moral obligation to do something about it.

My goal, to put it simply, was to turn Agent Orange from a source of antagonism and resentment into another example of the U.S. and Vietnamese governments working together to address one of the most difficult and emotional legacies of the war.[1]

Since 2007, the United States Congress has appropriated $231.2 million for the damages to human health and the environment attributed to dioxin. In 2011, Congress began appropriating separate amounts for environmental remediation and for health and disability programs in areas of Vietnam that were targeted by Agent Orange or were otherwise contaminated by dioxin. The foreign private sector, other governments, the United Nations Development Program, UNICEF and the Global Environmental Facility (GEF) have contributed $31.1 million.

Chart 7.1. Dioxin Cleanup and Health/Disabilities Services in Vietnam, 2007–2018 with Funding from the U.S. Government and Other Sources

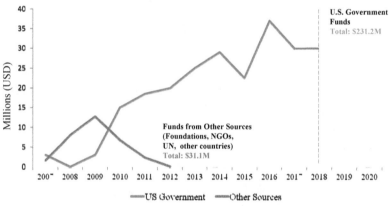

Non-U.S. government sources include Foundations (Ford Foundation, Atlantic Philanthropies, Gates Foundation, Nathan Cummings Foundation, Chino Cienega Foundation, and other U.S. Foundations,), Civic Groups, Businesses & Individuals, the UN, UNDP-GEF, US Fund for UNICEF, and the Governments of Canada, Czech Republic, Ireland, Netherlands, and Greece.

The United States Agency for International Development (USAID) has used most of the funds designated for dioxin remediation to clean up 90,000 cubic meters of dioxin-contaminated soils at the Da Nang Airport. When the project finishes in 2018, it is expected to have cost $108 million, with $105 million coming from the U.S. and $3 million coming from Vietnam. USAID has used the remainder of the funds

Table 7.1. U.S. Congress – Appropriations for Agent Orange/Dioxin in Vietnam
2007–2018

Year	Health & Disability Services ($ millions)	Dioxin Remediation ($ millions)	Total ($ millions)
2007	*	*	$3.0
2008	*	*	$0.0
2009	*	*	$3.0
2010	*	*	$15.0
2011	$3.0	$15.5	$18.5
2012	$5.0	$15.0	$20.0
2013	$4.8	$14.5	$19.3
2014	$7.0	$22.0	$29.0
2015	$7.5	$15.0	$22.5
2016	$7.0	$30.0	$37.0
2017	$10.0	$20.0	$30.0
2018	$10.0	$20.0	$30.0
State Department Allocations			$3.9
		Total	**$231.2**

* The total appropriation was divided between health & disabilities services and dioxin remediation from 2011 onward.

under this heading for an environmental impact assessment of the Bien Hoa Air Base and surrounding areas and technical assistance and training. Significant additional sums will be needed — on the order of $395 million to $500 million over ten years — to complete the remediation of the Bien Hoa Air Base.[2]

USAID's work on environmental remediation started in 2007, but its assistance for the disabled in Vietnam began in 1989 through the newly created Senator Patrick J. Leahy War Victims Fund. The program provided prosthetic and orthotic devices and physical rehabilitation for people who had come in contact with postwar unexploded ordnance, support for Vietnamese to manufacture and maintain the devices and for disability-related legislation. In 2007, the source of funding, the focus and the guideline for USAID's disability work underwent a sea change: the principal source of funds became annual appropriations from the U.S. Congress; the focus became one of the three Agent Orange/dioxin hot spots, Da Nang; and the guideline for assistance to the disabled "regardless of cause," was more strongly enunciated. From 2008 to 2015, USAID funded East Meets West Foundation, Save the Children and Vietnam Assistance for the Handicapped (VNAH) for work in Da Nang and then DAI (a U.S. international development company) for further work in Da Nang plus initiatives in the other two localities with dioxin hot spots, Bien Hoa and Phu Cat.[3] These projects combined some capacity building with direct services to people with disabilities in these locales. Other projects provided technical assistance for the National Law on Disability and related plans and regulations.

In 2015, USAID awarded funds to three Vietnamese nongovernment organizations and three non-Vietnamese NGOs for projects in six heavily sprayed provinces in the south — Thua Thien-Hue, Quang Nam, Binh Dinh, Dong Nai, Binh Phuoc and Tay Ninh — and Thai Binh, a province in the north that was never sprayed but where there are exceptionally large numbers of war veterans with children, grandchildren and great-grandchildren born with congenital malformities.

The following table shows the activities, the estimated numbers of disabled beneficiaries and the numbers of service providers to be trained under these six projects. The eighteen project activities are of three types:

1. Policy development — technical assistance for disability legislation and the development of policies, regulations, action plans and organizations for the benefit of disabled Vietnamese.
2. Capacity building — technical training for health care service providers at the provincial and district levels.
3. Direct services delivery of direct tangible assistance to people with disabilities and their caregivers.

Of the eighteen project activities, only three deliver direct services — tangible assistance to Vietnamese with disabilities and their caregivers. The other fifteen are for policy development and capacity building.

Several conclusions follow.

First, capacity enhancement and provision of direct services must go hand in hand. Assistance that just provides some services is unsustainable since all foreign aid eventually comes to an end. Assistance that focuses primarily on building capacity, without a way to test that capacity and accustom it to delivering services, is ineffective. Delivering services animates the capacity and increases the prospects that delivery of services will become self-sustaining. Effective development assistance needs to consciously balance the two.

And second, the U.S. Congress has provided these funds specifically to help Vietnamese impacted by Agent Orange/dioxin; it is a humanitarian response to a specific historical legacy entwining the U.S. and Vietnam. Under these circumstances USAID should allocate a more generous share of the funding to direct services and ensure that direct assistance and capacity building complement each other and prioritize Vietnamese impacted by Agent Orange/dioxin. The 2016 Appropriations Act provides such a way forward.

Since 2016, annual appropriations acts have prioritized disability funding to the Vietnamese provinces that were the most heavily sprayed with Agent Orange and then, within these, to severely disabled people.[4] USAID has used previous appropriations for services to everyone with a disability "regardless of cause." This meant that the available assistance was spread thinly and that Agent Orange victims only benefited randomly. It has never been USAID policy to single them out for accelerated attention nor indeed to recognize that they exist.

However, the 2016 spending bill states that "funds shall be made available for health and disability programs for areas sprayed with Agent Orange and otherwise contaminated with dioxin, to assist individuals with severe upper or lower body mobility impairments and/or cognitive or developmental disabilities."[5] These types of disabilities strongly correlate with people the Vietnamese deem Agent Orange victims.

From the Vietnamese perspective, this language means that a higher proportion of the available American assistance will reach the homes of such people to aid them and their caregivers and to build local capabilities.

From the State Department/USAID perspective, assistance channeled to the severely disabled could aim to assist everyone in that group "regardless of cause." American assistance to victims of unexploded ordnance has for many years helped everyone with a traumatic injury, whether or not it came from an unexploded bomb. Assistance to people with severe disabilities will work the same way.

The language in the spending bill thus frames the Agent Orange issue in a way that transcends politics and allows American humanitarian assistance to flow to Vietnam in a more focused way. With the 2016 Appropriations Act, Congress has created an opportunity for the two countries to take the next step together toward a breakthrough on Agent Orange.

Table 7.2. Allocation of $17.6 Million for Disability Projects in Vietnam
Source: USAID/Vietnam Project Briefs February 2017

NGO Recipient, Amount & Duration	Activities	Activity Type	Number of PWD Beneficiaries	Number of Service Providers & Caregivers Trained	Targeted Provinces
Viet Health $1.8 million 4 years	1. Train service providers/caregivers in early-childhood disability detection & intervention	(B) Capacity Building		4,000	Thai Binh, Tay Ninh
	2. Screen 140,000+ children for disabilities	(C) Direct Services	7,000 evaluated (including 1,000 interventions & 400 surgeries)		
Action for the Community Development Center (ACDC) $1.2 million 3 years	1. Train in leadership, life skills & advocacy for PWDs	(C) Direct Services		1,500	Thua Thien Hue, Binh Phuoc
	2. Help prepare provincial disability action plans	(A) Policy, Planning			
	3. Improve legal counseling for PWDs in rights & services	(B) Capacity Building		7,800	
	4. Increase public awareness on disabilities rights	(B) Capacity Building		9,000	
Disabilities Research & Development (DRD) $300,000 2.5 years	1. Increase public awareness of accessibility rights	(B) Capacity Building	20,000		Binh Dinh, Tay Ninh
	2. Audit accessibility & showcase model improvements	(B) Capacity Building	10 public buildings renovated		
	3. Train PWDs to advocate accessibility rights	(B) Capacity Building	300		

Table 7.2. Allocation of $17.6 Million for Disability Projects in Vietnam
Source: USAID/Vietnam Project Briefs February 2017 *(continued)*

NGO Recipient, Amount & Duration	Activities	Activity Type	Number of PWD Beneficiaries	Number of Service Providers & Caregivers Trained	Targeted Provinces
Vietnam Assistance for the Handicapped (VNAH) $5.9 million 5 years	1. Assist CRPD & national action plans, strengthen National Committee on Disability; roll out M&E framework; expand disability databases	(A) Policy, Planning			National
	2. Train rehab practitioners & occupational therapists	(B) Capacity Building		5,400	Binh Phuoc, Tay Ninh
	3. Equip provincial, district & commune rehab centers	(B) Capacity Building	4,000		
Handicapped International $5.4 million 5 years	1. Introduce medical/ rehab protocols for congenital brain defects & injuries	(B) Capacity Building	8,000		Thai Binh, Thua Thien Hue, Dong Nai; National
	2. Train med rehab & occupational/physical therapy	(B) Capacity Building		400	
	3. Impact measurement	(A) Policy, Planning			
Vietnam Veterans of America Foundation (VVAF) $3 million 5 years	1. Train service providers to maintain assistive devices	(B) Capacity Building		100	Thua Thien Hue, Binh Dinh, Quang Nam
	2. Provide assistive devices to PWDs	C) Direct Services	3,000		
	3. Disseminate information on rights, services & assistive devices	(B) Capacity Building			

CHAPTER EIGHT

What Do Agent Orange Victims Need?

Agent Orange victims have serious problems of mobility impairment and/ or cognitive disability and developmental delay. The most underserved of them live in poor and often remote communities, including upland areas and neighborhoods with heavy ethnic minority group populations. USAID in partnership with the government of Vietnam can best assist Agent Orange victims in the context of their families and communities — home improvements to enhance their mobility, parental respite and community rehabilitation centers, scholarships for their able-bodied sisters and brothers, and loans for family enterprises. Every family with a child or young adult with severe disabilities needs a threshold level of $1,000 worth of such in-kind services and investment to transform their prospects for a better life. Effective help to Agent Orange victims will be decisive for closer relations between Vietnam and the United States

T he previous two chapters described what the governments of Vietnam and the United States are doing for victims of Agent Orange. In this chapter we propose a "cooperative convergence" of these two initiatives to reach and assist more of the victims immediately and to strengthen Vietnamese institutions to sustain the assistance over time.

USAID has been assisting Vietnam with direct services and capacity building related to disability for many years. Irish Aid, UNICEF, the Ford and Rockefeller foundations, American companies and many individual donors have also provided aid. Among those whom these programs reach are people who were indirectly exposed to dioxin through a parent, grandparent or perhaps great-grandparent and are considered to be victims of Agent Orange.

They are people with very serious mental incapacity and mobility problems, living in poor and underserved communities and families, and somewhat remote from larger population centers. What do they need? They need support and services in the context of their families — such things as community respite care centers so their parents can get a break, scholarships so their able-bodied sisters and brothers can receive education, and loans for family enterprises.

We estimate that every child or young adult with severe disabilities needs at least $1,000 (2017 U.S. dollars) in services and investment in their family. In Vietnam such a level of help can totally transform the life of people living with disabilities and their families, especially if a victim is in an underserved rural area. USAID can aspire to reach and create new opportunity for tens of thousands of Vietnamese with disabilities. The challenge for the agency is to take Congressional appropriations for health and disability services, control intermediate costs and channel the funds through organizations with strong local structure and presence. This will maximize the impact on beneficiaries.

How can donors and their local partners most effectively reach such people and their families?

Tighten the Beneficiary Focus

For many Americans, including veterans of the war, the legacy of Agent Orange use in Vietnam remains a source of shame and moral outrage. And it remains an impediment to better U.S.-Vietnam relations. For both reasons, the United States should seek to reach those whom the Vietnamese public and leadership consider Agent Orange victims. We suggest several criteria for selecting future program beneficiaries. The criteria are operationally feasible. Applied consistently, these criteria will identify a beneficiary population significantly smaller than all people with disabilities, but which includes most Agent Orange victims. The criteria are:

> The person was born between 1965, when most of the spraying with Agent Orange began, and the present.

> *AND*

> The person's disability is the result of a birth defect or a defect that emerged spontaneously within the first fifteen years of his or her life.

> *AND EITHER*

> The person has mobility impairment, a mental disability or both.

> *OR*

> The person's disabilities are severe or very severe.

These selection criteria would encompass *most* of those whom the Vietnamese consider Agent Orange victims with disabilities. It would not include anyone born before 1965; they largely have health issues rather than disability issues. It would not include anyone born in 1965 or later with disabilities from accidents or other health conditions; these people are not regarded as Agent Orange victims. The one "hole" in this schema is apparently people born after 1965 who may have been exposed to dioxin at a hot spot and subsequently contracted a disease. In 2016, such people would be a maximum of fifty-one years old. Experience with war veterans in the United States suggests that some of these Vietnamese would not yet have manifested illnesses that U.S. law now regards as associated with dioxin exposure.

The larger issue is whether the United States government and/or the Vietnamese public and policymakers would regard this schema as too complicated and therefore hard to implement (United States) or as possibly excluding some legitimate claimants (Vietnam).

One alternative is to apply this framework not to *select individuals* for services, but rather as a way to *sort data* about people with disabilities from the 2009 Vietnam Population and Household Census. This approach would allow us to predict where the highest concentrations of Agent Orange victims are likely to be living. The United States (and perhaps other donors) would then work with the government of Vietnam to reach all of the people with disabilities in those districts.

Focus on families

Disabled people are more often than not poor, and they live in families that are poor. On the one hand, the families face unavoidable costs arising from special needs as well as the loss of income when an able-bodied adult family member has to stay home to give care. On the other hand, Vietnamese families are extremely strong and resilient. The best long-term prospects for most people with severe disabilities is to continue to live with their families rather than be moved into a long-term care facility (which in any event is unavailable in many rural areas).

Move to high-impact but underserved provinces

Up until now, American assistance has touched only people who live in towns and cities in the lowlands. The assistance now needs to pivot to the underserved rural and remote upland areas and ethnic minority groups. Vietnamese authorities and USAID can use the above profile of Agent Orange victims to prioritize districts within these provinces, reach everyone meeting the criteria and provide them and their families with services and assistance.

Deliver services and increase capacity simultaneously

Services and capacity-building need to be done together. This is the best way to meet the immediate need and to sustain services at a higher level once outside assistance inevitably ends.

Delivering services

Direct in-kind assistance is the best way to reach and transform the lives of Agent Orange victims. Properly designed, such assistance creates options and opportunities for the disabled person in the home and builds family assets. American assistance would be a one-time matter and tailored to the needs of the particular person and family. It would include, for example, rehabilitation therapies; equipment that enables the person with disabilities to be more mobile; accessibility improvements within the family home and around its compound; simple upgrades in water, sanitation and roofing; a scholarship for an able-bodied sibling to continue his or her schooling and investments in animal husbandry or tools for a trade for a family member. Such investments in families would strengthen them economically and enable them to better meet the continuing needs of the disabled family member over the longer run.

Building capacity

This includes both building more resilient families of those with severe disability and creating more competent social services that serve the disabled. The first priority for strengthening social services is to train large numbers of social workers with a specialty in disability services. Professional social workers are key to sustaining services for the severely disabled. Social workers will become the advocates for the severely disabled and their families and identify specific needs for specialized capacities and services the government of Vietnam should establish over the medium to long run. The findings of the provincial surveys of disabilities will be used to identify gaps and prioritize needs for the building of additional specialized capacities.

Follow the Vietnamese policy framework

The 2010 Vietnamese National Law on Disability and its implementing regulations give a practical framework for American assistance. These regulations now offer operational definitions of case management, individual care plan and other key concepts and tools. They define what disability is for purposes of providing public services and monthly allowances, and set performance standards. USAID can use the solid relationships that its support has built with the Vietnamese Ministry of Labor, Invalids and Social Affairs (MOLISA) at the national level to reach agreement on a multiyear plan for USAID assistance for disability services in the provinces. The goal of these efforts: when American and other international assistance come to an end, Vietnamese providers will have the capacity to meet the social, health and livelihood needs of Agent Orange victims and other people with disabilities.

Adapt the lessons of the Public-Private Partnership in Da Nang

In 2007, Hai Chau District in Da Nang introduced a case management system for its children living with disabilities. Known as the Hope System of Care, and assisted by Children of Vietnam, an American nongovernment organization, the initiative spread to other districts in the city. In 2010, American foundations, companies and the Aspen Institute — in collaboration with the People's Committee of Cam Le District — created a public-private partnership to introduce the Hope System of Care to the district. This experience produced the following lessons.

- Collaborate with and strengthen district-level government; providing social services in Vietnam is their responsibility.

- Enter a multiyear partnership with the district government to deliver services and expand capacity. The people's committee (local government) must seriously commit to take full budgetary responsibility for the enhanced services at the end of the defined period. Otherwise, there's no deal.

- Carry out a survey of individuals and families in the district to identify all people with severe disabilities as defined earlier, and create a database with this information. The database would be used to define the needs of the severely disabled, design appropriate responses and plan delivery of services.

- The partnership should adopt a case management approach and set up teams of case managers in each ward or commune. The case manager teams work with the individual and his or her family to create and update a care plan and then represent the individual in obtaining the required services. The partnership should also create interdisciplinary teams of service providers to provide expert recommendations for the individual care plans. The chair or vice chair of the people's committee in each ward or commune needs to be involved with the leadership and oversight of both kinds of teams.

- The partnership should deliver all the services to a disabled person that are called for in each care plan. In 2012–2013, the public-private partnership in Da Nang funded a suite of up to nine services for children and young adults with disabilities in Cam Le District. Fully implementing the service plan for each individual with disabilities creates a constituency of the recipient, his or her family and their neighbors. All of them will pressure the people's committee to continue the same standard of service after the end of the partnership with the donor.

- The partnership should create parent support groups for children with disabilities and strengthen disabled people's organizations (DPOs). Each can share experiences, resources and learning among members so they have the skills to advocate for their children and for themselves after the partnership with the donor ends.

- The partnership should enroll and map the locations of all the people with disabilities who meet the above criteria and live in the district. Each year it should survey the district, update enrollment, revise maps and update its database with newly arriving beneficiaries. This sets a precedent for inclusive and ongoing enrollment.

- It works best to select districts in high-impact provinces and close to districts that have already graduated from such a partnership, where possible, so that officials in both districts can regularly share experience.

- Capacities vary from place to place, so the partnership should consider adding other locally strong organizations such as the

Vietnam Red Cross, the Vietnam Association of Victims of Agent Orange/Dioxin (VAVA), parent support groups, DPOs and others.

In sum, the United States can demonstrate to the Vietnamese that America aims to help those whose lives have been damaged by Agent Orange. At the same time, this significant irritant to U.S.-Vietnam relations can be removed.

Survivors

Two sisters who are under the care of their mother
in Central Vietnam. *Courtesy of Ca Van Tran*

A young man who is being cared for by his family
in Central Vietnam. *Courtesy of Susan Hammond*

Areas Sprayed with Herbicides in Vietnam

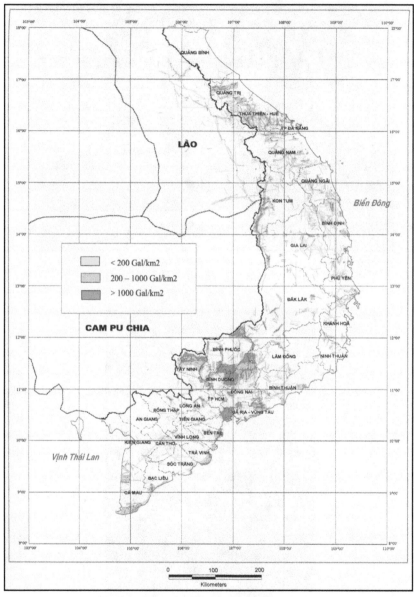

Figure 1. Areas in Vietnam sprayed with herbicides, 1961–1970, showing spraying intensities. *Courtesy of Ministry of Natural Resources and Environment, Office of National Steering Committee (Committee 33), Comprehensive Report, 2013 Hanoi, p. 9*

Total Area sprayed: 10,160 square miles (2,631,297 hectares)

Area sprayed with dioxin-contaminated herbicides:
6,486 square miles (1,679,734 hectares)

Total volume of herbicides:
19.5 million gallons (73,780,253 liters)

Volume of dioxin-contaminated herbicides:
12.6 million gallons (47,621,022 liters)

366 kilograms (807 pounds) of dioxin
released into the environment

Main staging areas:
U.S. air bases at Bien Hoa, Da Nang and Phu Cat

J.M. Stellman et al. "The extent and patterns of usage of Agent Orange and other herbicides in Vietnam," Nature, *April 2003, 422, 681–687.*

Contamination at Bien Hoa Air Base

Figure 2. Bien Hoa Air Base and surrounding city. Principal areas with dioxin-contaminated soils and pond sediments are shown in red. *Courtesy of Hatfield Consultants Partnership 2017.*

Despite warning signs, people continue to use ponds around the Bien Hoa
Air Base for raising fish and ducks. *Courtesy of Le Ke Son*

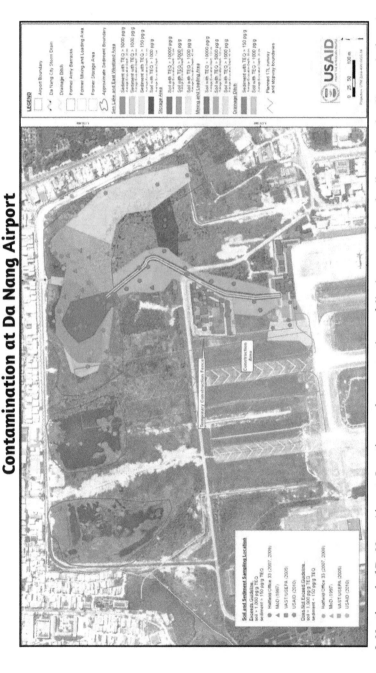

Figure 3. North end of Da Nang Airport. Locations and concentrations of dioxin-contaminated soils and pond sediments before the start of remediation in 2012. USAID/Vietnam, *Environmental Remediation at Da Nang Airport—Environmental Assessment, June 2010, p. 4.20.*

Area at the Da Nang Airport that was used to store drums of Agent Orange
and other herbicides during the 1960s, as it appeared before the start of
remediation in 2012. *Courtesy of Charles R. Bailey*

American Ambassador to Vietnam Michael Marine (blue necktie) at
the Da Nang Airport dioxin hot spot, July 24, 2007.
Courtesy of Le Ke Son

The Ford Foundation funded a concrete cap and drainage structures that immobilized the dioxin at the Da Nang Airport by January 2008. The heavy cap locked down the most contaminated soils and the structures channeled and trapped dioxin-laden sediments in storm water runoff pending the full remediation, which began in 2012. *Courtesy of Charles R. Bailey*

Left to right, front: Ambassador Ton Nu Thi Ninh and Walter Isaacson, co-chairs, U.S.-Vietnam Dialogue Group on Agent Orange/Dioxin. Rear: Jesper Morch, UNICEF representative in Vietnam, and John Hendra, U.N. resident coordinator in Vietnam, at the Da Nang Airport dioxin hot spot in June 2008. *Courtesy of Charles R. Bailey*

American Ambassador to Vietnam David B. Shear and
Vietnamese officials open the joint project to remediate the dioxin
at the Da Nang Airport, August 9, 2012. *Courtesy of Charles R. Bailey*

Left to right: Thomas G. Boivin, Hatfield Consultants, Ltd.; Ambassador Ha
Huy Thong, co-chair of U.S.-Vietnam Dialogue Group on Agent Orange/
Dioxin; Charles R. Bailey, and Le Ke Son at the launch of the dioxin
remediation project at the Da Nang Airport, August 9, 2012.
Courtesy of the authors

Containment structure being readied to treat dioxin-contaminated soil,
Da Nang Airport, May 2013. *Courtesy of Le Ke Son*

Left to right: American Ambassador to Vietnam David B. Shear,
U.S. Senator Patrick J. Leahy, Senior Lt. General Nguyen Chi Vinh,
Vietnam Ministry of Defense, and U.S.-Vietnam Dialogue Group co-chair
Ambassador Ha Huy Thong, at ceremonial opening of the dioxin remediation
plant at the Da Nang Airport, April 19, 2014. *Courtesy of Tim Rieser*

Dioxin-contaminated soils and pond sediments being
placed in a passive landfill at Phu Cat Airport, March 2012.
The project was completed on August 18, 2012. *Courtesy of Le Ke Son*

Dr. Nguyen Thi Ngoc Phuong is an important early researcher on dioxin
exposure and birth defects in Vietnam. *Courtesy of Le Ke Son*

A forest in Aluoi District, Thua Thien-Hue Province
in the 1970s, destroyed by Agent Orange. *Courtesy of Vo Quy*

Professor Vo Quy in 2016.
Courtesy of Le Ke Son

Professor Vo Quy conducting a
survey on the effects of Agent
Orange sprayed in the Nam Can
mangrove forests, 1970s.
Courtesy of Vo Quy

Phung Tuu Boi, director of the Center for Assistance in Nature Conservation and Community Development, initiated a project to plant "green fences" of honey locust trees with long thorns to keep people away from the dioxin hot spot in Aluoi. *Courtesy of Charles R. Bailey*

Dr. Le Van An, rector, Hue University of Agriculture and Forestry, operates a farm extension center in Aluoi District that introduces farmers to new techniques and opportunities in agroforestry. *Courtesy of Charles R. Bailey*

Ambassador Michael Marine in Washington, May 2015.
Courtesy of Le Ke Son

Left to right: The late Professor Vo Quy, a member of the
U.S.-Vietnam Dialogue Group; Tran Kim Chi, National Assembly staff
member; Ambassador Ngo Quang Xuan, the Dialogue Group co-chair; the late
Eni Faleomavaega, member, U.S. House of Representatives and chair,
Foreign Affairs Subcommittee on Asia and the Pacific; and Dialogue Group
member Do Hoang Long at the Agent Orange hearings, June 2009.
Courtesy of Charles R. Bailey

Left to right: Le Ke Son; Tim Rieser, Democratic Clerk,
Senate Appropriations Subcommittee on State and Foreign Operations;
and Charles R. Bailey in Washington, May 2015. *Courtesy of the authors*

Left to right: Susan V. Berresford, former president, Ford Foundation; Nguyen
Thi Hien, president, Vietnam Association for Victims of Agent Orange
(VAVA)/Da Nang; the late Bob Edgar, president, Common Cause; and disabled
youths at a vocational training center run by VAVA in Da Nang, March 2011.
Courtesy of Charles R. Bailey

Left to right: Charles R. Bailey; Ambassador Ngo Quang Xuan,
U.S.-Vietnam Dialogue Group co-chair; a local official; and two Dialogue
Group members, the late Professor Vo Quy and Do Hoang Long, inaugurate a
filtered water system in Dong Son Commune, Aluoi District, funded through
the U.S.-Vietnam Dialogue Group and Rotary International Foundation, March
2012. *Courtesy of Charles R. Bailey*

A young woman at the VAVA vocational training center,
Da Nang, April 2009. *Courtesy of Charles R. Bailey*

The parents of a child with disabilities confer with social workers in Da Nang in April 2012 under a project of the Cam Le District Peoples Committee and Children of Vietnam funded by private American foundations and businesses. *Courtesy of Truong Van Thom*

A child with physical and cognitive disabilities greets the new cow her family in Quang Nam Province received from the War Legacies Project in June 2017 through the support of the Bob Feldman Memorial Fund. Feldman was a Vietnam veteran from Minnesota. *Courtesy of Susan Hammond*

People with disabilities await medical examinations in Binh Phuoc Province in June 2017 as part of a project by Vietnam Assistance for the Handicapped (VNAH), funded by USAID. *Courtesy of Ca Van Tran*

Charles R. Bailey, center, and Le Ke Son interview Ambassador Le Van Bang, left, at his home in the Red River Delta, April 2015. *Courtesy of the authors*

Le Ke Son, center, and Charles R. Bailey interview James Zumwalt, left, at his home in Rehoboth Beach, Delaware, May 2015. *Courtesy of the authors*

Vietnam and the United States sponsor the screening of the 2016 Oscar-nominated film *Chau, Beyond the Lines* at the United Nations in New York, June 2016. The film, a landmark documentary, is about Le Minh Chau, a young man born with disabilities who struggles with the reality of his dream of becoming a professional artist. Left to right: Director Courtney Marsh, Le Minh Chau and Ambassador Nguyen Phuong Nga.
Courtesy of Nguyen Thanh Tuan

Le Minh Chau in his studio in Ho Chi Minh City.
Courtesy of Courtney Marsh

Can the Agent Orange Issue Be Resolved through the Courts in the U.S. or Elsewhere?

Many individuals and groups have sought to sue the chemical companies and the United States government for the manufacture and use of dioxin-contaminated herbicides in Vietnam during the war. American veterans achieved a pretrial settlement of their suit in 1984. It was the largest class-action suit filed up to that time. Vietnamese Agent Orange victims sued the chemical companies in 2004 but were unsuccessful. Scientific complexities, the unsettled causal relationship between dioxin exposure and ill health and disability and the challenges of proof under American tort law stand in the way of a legal solution to the legacy of Agent Orange. Any future law-suits will encounter similar dead ends.

O ver the decades since the end of the Vietnam War, many individuals and organizations have demanded that the United States Government and the chemical companies pay compensation for the damages to human health and well-being and the harm to the environment arising from the use of Agent Orange. The United States has never agreed that it has a legal duty to provide funds or assistance to remediate the harms caused by Agent Orange. On the other hand, since 1991 the United States has provided benefits to American veterans of the Vietnam War suffering from illnesses related to dioxin. Monsanto, Dow Chemical and the other chemical companies that produced Agent Orange did agree to an out-of-court settlement that resulted in a fund of $330 million for veterans in the United States, Australia and New Zealand.

Since 2007, the United States Congress has appropriated $231.2 million for assistance to people with disabilities in Vietnam and for remediation of dioxin hot spots. Thus, although both the United States Government and the chemical companies have never used the term compensation or reparations, and have never formally admitted liability, they have performed some acts of humanitarian responsibility. Other countries that participated in the Vietnam war, especially Australia, New Zealand and South Korea, also have had similar arrangements.

These are complex issues facing the plaintiffs who are victims of Agent Orange in Vietnam. First, the American chemical companies manufactured Agent Orange under contract to the United States. The use of Agent Orange in Vietnam was the result of decisions taken over three presidencies and five Congresses. It impacted not only the Vietnamese plaintiffs, but also American veterans and United States allies who participated in the Vietnam War. A legal solution to this issue has been and will continue to be near impossible to reach due to the complex science of causation and the demands of proof under American tort law. Alternative pathways need to be pursued so that the United States and the chemical companies that produced the herbicides can enlarge their regard for and humanitarian assistance to those affected by dioxin.

American Veterans

In 1977, American veterans of the Vietnam War began to file claims with the Department of Veterans Affairs for disability payments and health care for illnesses, miscarriages and birth defects they believed were caused by exposure to dioxin while they served in Vietnam.

Veterans Affairs, however, denied their claims unless they could prove that the condition began while they were in the service or within one year thereafter and held to the position that dioxin had only short-term and reversible effects on human health. In February 1979, some 52,220 American veterans of the war and their families filed a class-action suit against six of the chemical companies that had produced Agent Orange for the United States Department of Defense.[1]

The case was heard by Judge Jack Weinstein in the United States District Court for the Eastern District of New York.[2] Judge Weinstein defined the class as all veterans who served in Vietnam between 1961 and 1972 from the United States, Australia and New Zealand who believed that they or their children had been harmed by dioxin. Both sides ultimately agreed to a pretrial settlement of $180 million. Judge Weinstein established the Agent Orange Settlement Fund with the money and asked Kenneth Feinberg to create a plan to disburse it.[3]

With interest, the settlement fund ultimately grew to $330 million. The disbursement plan had two components, a Payment Program and a Class Assistance Program. The Payment Program disbursed $205 million through compensation payments to 52,000 totally disabled American veterans and survivors of deceased veterans.[4] The awards averaged about $3,900 each. The Class Assistance Program distributed $74 million to 83 social service nongovernment organizations throughout the United States to provide counseling, medical and case management services to 239,000 veterans and their families. With legal costs, the fund had fully distributed its assets by September 1997, and Judge Weinstein ordered it closed.[5]

Reflecting back on the case in 2016, Feinberg remarked:

> Weinstein looked at all the scientific and medical evidence — all of it. He agonized over it. He concluded the following: No individual in a court [bearing] the burden of proof can demonstrate by a preponderance of the evidence — 51 percent — that their illness or injury was caused by Agent Orange herbicide exposure in Vietnam. It doesn't matter whether it's a Vietnamese citizen, a domestic citizen, a soldier, nobody — according to Judge Weinstein based on the medical evidence in 1984. That ruling has not changed to this day.. . . However, [Judge Weinstein did find] as a matter of law that the plaintiffs have demonstrated that as a class

[he could] find no other explanation except that it's Agent Orange. That's why he accepted the settlement.

Weinstein's ruling in [this] case set the benchmark for all subsequent legal discussions of a judge, in terms of government liability, in terms of medical scientific causation, [and] in terms of methodologies for compensating eligible victims. That benchmark decision, affirmed by the Second Circuit Court of Appeals, which the Supreme Court of the United States declined to review, ended for all intents and purposes any legal discussion in the United States about Agent Orange.[6]

While the lawsuit was underway, some veterans sought to get the United States Congress to act on their concerns. Veterans began to mobilize, and in 1978 Bobby Muller and others formed Vietnam Veterans of America.[7] Over the next decade, Congress approved funds for epidemiological studies and health care, and in 1991, Congress passed the Agent Orange Act, which provides compensation to American veterans who served in Vietnam and later developed any of a growing list of illnesses and conditions.[8]

Vietnamese Agent Orange Victims

By 2003, many in Vietnam had become frustrated that the United States was doing nothing for Vietnamese victims of Agent Orange even as the United States government ramped up compensation for American veterans who had become ill from their exposure to Agent Orange in Vietnam. A small group of Vietnamese doctors, scientists and retired military officers decided to sue those responsible. They formed VAVA to protect the interests of victims and raise funds for their care. Other members are individuals and groups who have volunteered to assist the victims.

In the United States, the federal government has sovereign immunity and may not be sued without its consent. Consequently VAVA and twenty-seven named individuals[9] filed suit on January 30, 2004, against the chemical companies and their subsidiaries and affiliates that had produced Agent Orange.[10]

The Vietnamese case began on March 18, 2004, in the United States District Court for the Eastern District of New York before Judge Jack

Weinstein, the same judge who'd heard the American veterans' Agent Orange lawsuit twenty years earlier. The Vietnamese side argued that as a direct result of the defendants' actions, the plaintiffs had suffered physical injuries, pain and suffering, severe mental anguish and loss of livelihoods. They also charged that the defendants' actions contaminated the environment. The plaintiffs asked the court for compensatory and punitive damages "in amounts to be proven at trial" and a court order requiring the defendants to pay for environmental remediation in Vietnam.[11] The plaintiffs further asserted that the defendants had violated customary international law.[12]

The chemical companies moved to dismiss the case. They argued that the statute of limitations had expired, that the court lacked jurisdiction, that the plaintiffs' request for the companies to fund the remediation of dioxin was infeasible and that court oversight of remediation would infringe on Vietnam's sovereignty and impact U.S. foreign policy in Vietnam. The companies also asserted that the case would violate the "political question" doctrine.[13] Most importantly for the case, the companies asserted that the plaintiffs had failed to establish a claim that the chemical companies had violated international laws.

At the request of Weinstein, the United States Department of Justice submitted an amicus brief ("Statement of Interest") in which the government argued that the court has no authority to pass on the validity of the president's decisions regarding combat tactics and weaponry, made as commander in chief of the United States during a time of active combat. Moreover, before deciding to use herbicides, the executive branch had considered and found no international or international customs against this tactic. Prior to April 1975, the United States had not approved the 1925 Geneva Protocol and therefore was not bound to this protocol. Article 23 (a) of the 1907 Hague Convention is applicable to toxic chemicals and not to defoliants and herbicides. The United States government was also concerned about setting a precedent, asserting: "The implications of plaintiffs' claims are astounding, as they would (if accepted) open the courthouse doors of the American legal system to former foreign enemy nationals and soldiers claiming to have been harmed by the United States Armed Forces' use of materials supplied by American manufacturers during times of war."[14]

On March 10, 2005, Judge Weinstein issued a 233-page decision to dismiss the case. These three major legal issues barred the way to a successful suit by Vietnamese victims of Agent Orange against the chemical companies:

United States Domestic Law

The court dismissed all claims brought by the Vietnamese under American domestic law because of the government (military) contractor defense. The contractor defense doctrine shields private contractors from tort liability associated with their performance of government procurement contracts. It covers all domestic state and federal substantive law claims.[15] The doctrine says, in essence, "The government told us to do it and knew at least as much as we did about the dangers."[16] The plaintiffs asserted that the chemical companies withheld information from the United States government on the dioxin levels in their herbicides. Judge Weinstein found that the government knew at least as much or more than the chemical companies about their product.

International Law

The contractor defense cannot be used to counter claims brought under international law. An international law claim was thus the plaintiff's strongest strategy. The court ruled that to establish the chemical companies' liability under international law, the plaintiffs would need to show (a) that the usage was illegal under international law, (b) that the defendants knew how their product would be used and (c) that they supplied the product, becoming a party to the illegality. Judge Weinstein found that (b) and (c) could be shown but not (a). He wrote, "Detailed analysis of international law claims of the Vietnamese plaintiffs establishes that use of herbicides by or on behalf of the United States in Vietnam before 1975 was not a violation of international law."[17] Weinstein found that "chemicals designed and used as herbicides to kill plants, as defendants' products were designed and used during the Vietnam War, are not outlawed as 'poison or poisonous weapons' under even the broadest interpretation of that phrase."[18] Moreover, he wrote, "The herbicides were not 'calculated to cause unnecessary suffering.'

The herbicide spraying was in the course of armed activities deemed necessary by the United States to protect American armed forces and those of its allies. It was not designed to harm people or land independently as a punishment or to inflict hurt viciously and consciously."[19] In consequence, he ruled, many areas of international law such as torture, war crimes and genocide do not apply in this case since they all require demonstrated harmful intent. The tension, or contradiction, between the two holdings — that the chemical companies and the United States government had the knowledge but not the intent — was left unresolved.

Causality

Judge Weinstein's rulings were sufficient to dismiss the case based on the plaintiff's claims under domestic and international laws. He made it clear, however, that any future litigation claiming dioxin exposure and subsequent ill health would face formidable barriers under U.S. tort law: scientific evidence would need to demonstrate a connection more probable than not, each plaintiff would need to prove exposure and every plaintiff would need to trace the links between the dioxin produced by specific companies and the resulting harm he or she directly experienced.[20]

Weinstein wrote:

- "Proof of causal connection depends primarily upon substantial epidemiological and other scientific data, particularly since some four million Vietnamese are claimed to have been adversely affected. Anecdotal evidence of the kind charged in the complaint . . . cannot suffice to prove cause and effect."[21]

- "No study or technique presented to the court has demonstrated how it is now possible to connect the herbicides supplied by any defendant to exposure by any plaintiff to dioxin from that defendant's herbicide."[22]

The Vietnamese appealed to the United States Court of Appeals for the Second Circuit in New York, asking the court to reverse the decision by Judge Weinstein. The appellate court dismissed the appeal. A rehearing by an expanded (en banc) panel of appellate judges confirmed Judge Weinstein's decision on May 7, 2008. The plaintiffs then petitioned the United States Supreme Court for a writ of certiorari to hear the case.

In their petition to the Supreme Court, the plaintiffs defined the central point at issue as follows:

> This case is not and has never been about whether the manufacture, supply and use of **herbicides** [emphasis in original] per se to defoliate large areas of Viet Nam violated customary international law. Rather, it is about whether the use of herbicides which respondents knew contained excessive and avoidable amounts of poison (dioxin) and which added nothing to the defoliations process, violated customary international law. . . . The crux of the court of appeal's holding was that since the government's intent was not to spray a poison on humans, and that the dioxin contamination was an 'unintended' consequence of spraying Agent Orange, there was not a sufficient level of intent necessary to demonstrate a violation of customary international law. Petitioners allege otherwise in their amended complaint, at least insofar as the chemical company respondents are concerned.[23]

In March 2009, the Supreme Court denied the plaintiffs' petition for a writ of certiorari to hear an appeal. This decision brought to an end further recourse to United States courts for redress of American use of Agent Orange in Vietnam.

South Korean Veterans of the Vietnam War

Over 300,000 South Korean soldiers served in Vietnam between 1965 and 1972, and many of them were exposed to the spraying of Agent Orange. The 1984 Agent Orange Settlement Fund, however, did not cover the South Koreans, even though it did apply to veterans in the United States, Australia and New Zealand.

In 1999, some 20,000 South Korean Vietnam War veterans filed two class action suits against Monsanto and Dow Chemical in the Seoul District Court, seeking $4.4 billion in damages. The District Court ruled against them in 2002.[24] They appealed and in early 2006 the Seoul High Court overturned the lower court's decision, requiring the chemical companies to compensate 6,795 veterans in the amount of $61 million.

The chemical companies appealed to the Supreme Court of Korea, which gave its decision on July 12, 2013. Korea's highest court reversed the ruling of the Seoul High Court except for thirty-nine veterans with chloracne, a severe but treatable skin disorder, for which the court found evidence of causality and ordered the chemical companies to pay $415,000 in damages.[25] The Supreme Court sent the case of the other veterans back to the appeals court, saying in a statement, "There is no evidence their diseases were caused by their exposure to defoliant spray during the Vietnam War."[26] The thirty-nine plaintiffs now face the question of how they can get the judgment obtained in South Korea enforced against the chemical companies in the United States.

The narrowness of the Korean court ruling — it benefits only thirty-nine Korean war veterans suffering one disease — suggests that the Korean case will not eventually prompt United States courts to reverse thirty years of legal decisions adverse to victims of Agent Orange.

How Has the Bilateral Relation on Agent Orange Changed Over Time, and What Is the Situation Today?

United States' spraying of Agent Orange on a massive scale in Vietnam was a historic mistake, and the legacy of ill health and disability that followed has been a disaster for both countries. The governments of the two countries could not agree on what to do about Agent Orange even after diplomatic relations were established in 1995, until a breakthrough occurred in 2006. Vietnamese readiness and initiatives from the U.S. Embassy, Congress and the Ford Foundation led to the breakthrough. Vietnam and the United States have developed a strong partnership in cleaning up the dioxin at two former U.S. military bases. Congress has directed that U.S. health and disability assistance go to the most severely disabled living in the provinces that were sprayed. These U.S. actions since 2007 have notably strengthened relations with Vietnam across the board.

The American use of herbicides in Vietnam during the war was a historic mistake by the United States, and its lingering legacies of ill health and disabilities since then have been a disaster for both countries. It has taken decades for the United States and Vietnam to move from no discussion of the issue to limited talks to joint action on cleaning dioxin residues at former American military bases of the legacy of Agent Orange. There has been less progress on United States help for the Vietnamese suffering ill health and coping with disabilities linked to direct and indirect exposure to the dioxin in Agent Orange. American assistance for the disabled has been delivered "regardless of cause" and therefore lacks the sharp focus needed to reach the people whom the Vietnamese regard as victims of Agent Orange. Beginning in 2015 annual appropriations acts approved in Washington sharpened the focus of official American disability assistance to Vietnam. Appropriations acts since then stipulate that funds will go to projects and programs in areas that were heavily sprayed and, within these areas, to people with severe physical and mental disabilities.

The impact of Agent Orange, beyond its defoliation of trees and other vegetation, took decades to unfold. The United States embargo of Vietnam lasted twenty years, from 1975 to 1995. During this period there was no diplomatic relationship and therefore little official contact between the two governments. Action on the legacy of Agent Orange proceeded on quite separate tracks in Vietnam and in the United States.

Dr. Le Cao Dai was a Hanoi surgeon and veteran of Vietnam's struggle against French colonialism after World War II. During the Vietnam War he directed a field hospital in the Central Highlands within South Vietnam to treat North Vietnamese troops. From 1966 to 1974, Dr. Dai's hospital was forced to relocate whenever American planes sprayed Agent Orange to defoliate the forests that concealed northern forces. Dr. Dai and everyone in the area could see that Agent Orange defoliated the trees, but they had no reason to know that the herbicide was contaminated with dioxin, nor could they foresee the consequences of dioxin exposure for their health. By the early 1970s, Dr. Dai and other Vietnamese doctors began seeing soldiers suffering from unusual diseases. They also noticed numerous miscarriages, premature births and birth defects among soldiers' children. In October 1980, the government of Vietnam set up the 10-80 Committee in the Ministry of Health with Dr. Hoang Dinh Cau as director and Dr. Dai as deputy director. Over the next fifteen years, the 10-80 Committee led Vietnamese efforts to understand and respond to the Agent Orange legacy.

Vietnamese scientists made early contributions. Before the war ended, Professor Vo Quy, a biologist at Vietnam National University in Hanoi, surveyed the damage the herbicide spraying had done to the forests and wildlife in the upland areas of South Vietnam and reported back to the government in Hanoi. After the war, a renowned surgeon, Professor Ton That Tung, compared the medical histories of soldiers who had gone south with those who had not. He found a dramatic increase in rates of cancers and birth defects in the children of those who had gone to the south.

On the American side, in the early 1980s a Vietnam veteran, Bobby Muller, emerged as a spokesman of American Vietnam veterans. As president of Vietnam Veterans of America, Muller articulated a growing concern among veterans that their exposure to Agent Orange was the cause of significant health problems that so many veterans were having. As Muller later related, "This was a problem. People were dying young. . . . Health consequences were traumatic." United States officials said that they did not know which troops were specifically sprayed and that therefore it would not be possible to show the consequences of exposure. Muller countered, "Well, O.K., but Vietnam is where this stuff was used. There is no question. People have been living there. That's the laboratory. If we look at the consequences for Vietnamese people whom we know have had exposure, that will inform our process." Muller concluded, "As the head of Vietnam Vets, nobody was in a better position to do an outreach to Vietnam than the leadership of those who fought. Politicians are not going to get ahead of us who fought in the war and paid the price."[1]

Accordingly, Muller led a small group of American veterans in 1982 to Hanoi, where they met with Dr. Tung, who told them, "The dramatic increases in birth defects and cancers don't make sense because we're not industrialized, we don't have major manufacturing with pollutants and toxins. That's not an explanation for this dramatic increase in birth defects and illnesses we're seeing among those who operated in defoliated areas. We'll do whatever we can to work with you."[2]

From 1968 to 1970, Admiral Elmo R. Zumwalt Jr. commanded United States naval forces patrolling the coasts, harbors and rivers of South Vietnam. He ordered Agent Orange sprayed over the Mekong Delta to kill vegetation along the waterways and reduce ambushes. His son, Lieutenant Elmo Zumwalt III, who served in Vietnam 1969-70, commanded one of the Navy boats patrolling the rivers. In 1977, Elmo III's son, Elmo IV, was born with a severe learning disability. Six years later, Elmo III was diagnosed with cancer, from which he died in 1988 at the age of forty-two. Admiral Zumwalt and his son attributed the cancer and the boy's learning disability to Agent Orange.[3]

In 1990, Admiral Zumwalt carried out a study that connected dioxin exposure with twenty-five kinds of cancers. His findings contradicted earlier evaluations by the Department of Veterans Affairs that showed no correlation. The United States Congress created an independent scientific review panel in 1991 in the Institute of Medicine that since then has identified seventeen cancers and other illnesses associated with dioxin exposure. Zumwalt and his younger son, James Zumwalt, visited Hanoi in 1994 as private citizens. James Zumwalt said of his father:

> He realized it was important to get the two governments working together, so he went over there with the purpose of trying to get the U.S. government and the Vietnamese government to do a study on the Agent Orange issue.
>
> The Vietnamese had not yet decided how they wanted to handle the issue. The U.S. government made no effort to show there was interest on their side to do this study. The trip had all good intentions but didn't make the progress we had hoped it would make.[4]

Matters moved ahead in the United States, however. In May 1996, President Bill Clinton held a news conference on Agent Orange's impact on American veterans. Admiral Zumwalt was present as the president announced that the United States would "take further steps to ease the suffering our nation unintentionally caused its own sons and daughters by exposing them to Agent Orange in Vietnam." Clinton continued: "For over two decades, Vietnam veterans made the case that exposure to Agent Orange was injuring and killing them long before they left the field of battle, even damaging their children. For years, the government did not listen. . . . [W]ith the important step we are taking today, we are showing that America can listen and act." The president then announced that veterans "are entitled to disability payments based upon their exposure to Agent Orange. Our administration will also propose legislation to meet the needs of veterans' children afflicted with the birth defect spina bifida — the first time the offspring of American soldiers will receive benefits for combat-related health problems."[5]

It would take more than a decade — until 2007 — for the United States government to really start to come to grips with the legacy of Agent Orange in Vietnam itself. According to former Ambassador Le Van Bang, between 1986 and 1994, "The relations between Vietnam and the United States [were] so difficult that we could not talk about anything except MIAs and POWs."[6] In 1989, Foreign Minister Nguyen Co Thach asked the United States to form another team to talk about humanitarian issues of Vietnam and assigned Le Van Bang to lead the Vietnamese side. The team called for prosthetic devices for wounded veterans and others in the countryside. Bang recalled, "That was the number-one issue [where] the United States could help us. And when we talked about other issues, Agent Orange or the victims of it, the United States refused to hear. 'No, no, we are not talking about that one. If you talk about that one we [will] go away.' . . . They all said it was the policy of the U.S. Government, the Administration."[7]

As the Vietnamese continued to work with U.S. officials, they also reached out to American nongovernmental organizations and invited them to start programs in Vietnam. The Ford Foundation, a leading American philanthropy, received such an invitation in 1991 and began making a small number of grants in international relations, social science research and women's studies from its offices in Bangkok. In 1993 Susan V. Berresford, then the Ford Foundation program vice president, visited Hanoi to meet officials, scientists and others to learn about further needs in these areas. At the end of her official schedule, her hosts asked if she would be willing to stop at a hospital. Although the Ford Foundation does not support healthcare work, she agreed. There she was shown evidence of birth defects and the officials said they hoped the foundation would help with Agent Orange. Berresford replied that the foundation would think about it. The Ford Foundation went ahead with its grant making in Vietnam and three years later opened a representative office in Hanoi. To the new representative, Charles Bailey, Berresford suggested that he keep alert for how the foundation might get engaged in a useful way with Agent Orange.

In 1993, Vice Foreign Minister Vu Khoan made his first visit to the United States on a study tour funded by the Ford Foundation. He later said, "That very trip opened my getting to know the U.S." In 1995 he was put in charge of relations with the U.S. In 2015 he said:

> To be honest, at that time I could not imagine then that the relationship between the U.S. and Vietnam could develop as far as [it has] today. When the BTA [bilateral trade agreement] was signed, trade between the two countries was $780 million, and now it's $40 billion — such a big jump, I could not imagine that big jump. Everybody asked why so [fast]? Let me go back to the history.
>
> Everybody knows that the relation between the two countries underwent a very unfortunate history, causing pain to both countries and many children of the two countries died during the war, damaging the relation which should have been good [and] causing complicated problems in the region. Why was that? I want to be frank; that may be because the U.S. got wrong signals. . . . [D]uring the Second World War, our President Ho Chi Minh and General Vo Nguyen Giap showed strong gestures to become friends with the U.S. After the August revolution was successful and the new State of Vietnam came into being, Ho Chi Minh wrote fourteen times to the U.S. president and to the secretary of state while he wrote only twice to Stalin, but he did not receive positive feedbacks from the U.S. That's the first mistake of the U.S., which opened up a series of mistakes that came later, let alone the history after 1945. Many opportunities were missed. The unfortunate happenings caused the history of relations between the two countries to lose decades.
>
> What happened was unreasonable, but the normalization of relations is reasonable. When the relation was put on the right track, it developed fast. [T]he U.S. is also an Asia-Pacific country [and its] trade and business are a large proportion in the Asia-Pacific region. It's not by accident that the U.S. joined the Pacific war because its interest was linked with this region and during World War II, the real threat to the U.S. came from this region. So the U.S.'s interest in this region is inevitable.
>
> Vietnam has an important geo-economic and geopolitical position in this region. I say this not because I am a Vietnamese; you can just look at the map and can see [this] right away. . . . The fact that conflicts in the region have involved Vietnam shows the important position of Vietnam. In the Second World War, the

Japanese came here, the French had a war here for nine years, [the American] war was here for ten years, later other people's war was also here. Our sufferings themselves tell our important role.

Economically speaking, Vietnam is a poor country [and] doesn't have a significant role, but for the future, for the development of the region, Vietnam is absolutely an important destination. Mutual benefits meet. We can share benefits, of course, not to be against anybody, but for development. This is a factor in that fast development. Secondly, we suffered wars the most in the world. No countries but one country in Europe and Vietnam have seen a Thirty Years' War.[8] So our nation's aspiration to get out of poverty is strong. We really need an environment and a partner to develop. One of the foremost important partners is the U.S. itself.[9]

Vietnamese officials in the North were well aware of the wartime spraying of Agent Orange, but after the war ended they faced many other challenges and the government did not have the resources and capacity to study the issue. As the Vietnamese collected more information, however, the more they realized its seriousness. They also realized that in the process of normalization, Khoan said, adding, "There were many big issues of strategic significance — regional, political and economic relations. We focused on the big issues first — normalization of relations. We didn't want to do anything that might hinder the process."[10]

Normalization did move forward: On February 3, 1994, President Bill Clinton lifted the trade embargo against Vietnam, and on January 25, 1995, Vietnam and the United States signed an agreement settling all claims of each country, and nationals of each country, "arising from the nationalization, expropriation, or taking of, or other measures directed against, properties, rights and interests" of the other.[11] On July 11, 1995, President Clinton announced the United States would establish ambassadorial-level relations with Vietnam. In April 1997 Pete Peterson, a former Vietnam War POW and Member of Congress, became U.S. ambassador to Vietnam.

In October 1997, Le Van Bang, now the Vietnamese ambassador to the United States, accompanied Foreign Minister Nguyen Manh Cam to meet Secretary of State Madeleine Albright. Cam thought that it was time to talk about Agent Orange. They quickly learned that the State Department message was, "We are not talking about it and we will tell the press that we, both of us, Vietnam and the United States — didn't talk about this issue during our discussion today."[12] American diplomats posted to Hanoi in the late 1990s were instructed never to use the phrase Agent Orange.[13]

The Vietnamese concluded that if they couldn't move the bilateral relationship forward on other fronts, then they couldn't talk about Agent Orange with the United States. Nevertheless, Vietnam continued to raise the issue in high-level official meetings — Deputy Defense Minister Tran Hanh with Defense Secretary William Cohen during Hanh's visit to the United States in October 1998, Prime Minister Phan Van Khai with President Clinton at the Asia-Pacific summit in New Zealand in September 1999 and Foreign Affairs Minister Nguyen Dy Nien with Ambassador Peterson in March 2000. According to Lewis M. Stern, the former director for Southeast Asia at the Defense Department, "The U.S. Government response to Vietnamese insistence on the primacy of a bolder, larger, more mainstream USG effort to heal the wounds of war emphasized the practical and budgetary difficulties, the potentially politically crippling consequences, and the rational and organizational impediments to moving in the direction the Vietnamese suggested."[14]

In April 2000, Charles Bailey, then the Ford Foundation representative in Vietnam, responding to a request from the Vietnam Red Cross, allocated $150,000 to the Red Cross Agent Orange Victims Fund. In an internal memo Bailey wrote that this action "would be well appreciated by the Vietnamese — for the actual value of the funds and, more importantly, for the recognition given to the disabled and for the encouragement the Foundation's contribution will give to other donors. The Vietnam Red Cross reports that the American Red Cross is planning a contribution of $350,000 to the Fund this year, with an additional $1 million over the next two years. These donations also come at a time in the Vietnam-U.S. relationship when positive and constructive actions are especially needed."[15]

In November 2000, President Bill Clinton visited Vietnam. He met Le Kha Phieu, secretary-general of the Communist Party of Vietnam, who raised the Agent Orange issue. American presidents are *ex officio* presidents of the American Red Cross, and it was in that capacity that Clinton went to see Professor Nguyen Trong Nhan, president of the

Vietnam Red Cross Society. Before the meeting, Professor Nhan laid out the issue in a letter to Clinton:

> The Agent Orange victims in Vietnam are numerous; their number is being estimated at around 1 million. They lead a miserable life. It is very much disturbing that the effects of the dioxin are taking toll on their grandchildren's generation. . . . May I propose to you, Mr. President, given your . . . commitment to restore the normal relationship with Vietnam, to take humanitarian measures to help the Vietnam Red Cross address the plight of the Agent Orange victims both in terms of material and psychological support. Furthermore, the U.S. Government might consider the cooperation with Vietnam in clearing the dioxin-affected areas to lessen the damage to the local people. I [also] recommend that the scientific research on this issue should be promoted between our two countries and even include experts from other countries in order to prevent the hereditary damages to the future generations and even to identify and cure the illnesses caused by the Agent Orange.[16]

Clinton replied two and a half months later: "Thank you for your moving letter expressing your thoughts regarding the Vietnamese victims of Agent Orange. I share many of your concerns about the medical and psychological difficulties that they face and I agree with the need for scientific research and joint humanitarian efforts between our two nations."[17] But Clinton was no longer president, and the American Red Cross moved on. At the end of its three-year, $1.35 million grant, it declined further support to the Vietnam Red Cross Agent Orange Fund. Bailey learned from the experience of the Ford Foundation and American Red Cross grants that responding to the human impact of Agent Orange would require on the one hand far larger resources than the Ford Foundation possessed and on the other that scaling up assistance from other donors would be no easy task.

The United States continued to maintain there was no credible scientific evidence linking dioxin exposure to ill health and birth defects but agreed to a meeting of scientists to examine the issue in Singapore in November 2000. Pham Khoi Nguyen, deputy minister of the Ministry of Science, Technology and the Environment and deputy head of Committee 33, led the nineteen-member Vietnamese delegation. Dr. Kenneth Olden, director of the National Institute of Environmental Health

Sciences (NIEHS), headed the United States delegation of sixteen people. The Vietnamese side put forward proposals for research, support to Agent Orange victims, treatment facilities for victims and the cleanup of dioxin in heavily polluted areas. The United States side said that the meeting was only to advise on scientific cooperation and that it was not authorized to address other matters. As a result, the meeting came to a standstill and ended with the two sides unable to sign any document, not even a record of their discussions. The first official meeting of the two governments on Agent Orange had failed; the two sides were poles apart.

Discussions continued, however, and in July 2001, the American ambassador, Pete Peterson, told the *Vietnam News*, "The U.S. has long offered to engage in serious, joint scientific research with Vietnam to reach a well-founded understanding of the environmental and health effects of dioxin, an element in Agent Orange that has been claimed to cause health problems."[18]

In March 2002, the two sides met again, this time at the Daewoo Hotel in Hanoi in a scientific conference on the effects of Agent Orange/ dioxin on human health and the environment. Some 120 American and other foreign scientists presented thirty-two papers and twenty-seven reports in poster format. Vietnamese participants included 280 scientists and representatives from several agencies; the scientists presented thirty papers and seven reports in poster format. The topics were far ranging: methods to measure the impact of dioxin on the environment, remediation techniques, harm-reduction measures and the effects of dioxin on reproductive health and its links to cancers and other changes in human biology. Some papers, particularly those on health impacts, reached differing and even contradictory conclusions.

Dr. Nguyen Ngoc Sinh, director of both the Vietnam Environmental Agency and the Office of Committee 33, and Dr. Anne P. Sassaman, director of Extramural Research and Training at the National Institute of Environmental Health Sciences, headed the respective official delegations. The two delegations met following the conference and agreed to three areas of cooperation over the next year: an epidemiological study comparing birth defects among Vietnamese women in sprayed and unsprayed areas, a bilateral technical committee to confer annually on scientific and technical matters (later known as the Joint Advisory Committee, or JAC) and technical cooperation on dioxin measurement in soils and sediments at the Vietnam Academy of Science and Technology (VAST).

The State University of New York at Albany and the Hanoi Medical University were to jointly conduct the epidemiological study. However, the Americans and Vietnamese were unable to agree on its design and conduct, and the study was canceled by the U.S. National Institute of Environmental Health Sciences in March 2005. Each side blamed the other for the failure. David Carpenter, director of the Institute for Health and the Environment at Albany and who was involved with planning the study, later said he believed that it made both sides uncomfortable because "U.S. officials worried that if we associated birth defects with dioxin, then we'd be liable for reparations [and] the Vietnamese worried that if we didn't make that association, they'd lose the propaganda benefits of blaming us for the birth defects."[19] The JAC, agreed on in 2002, met for the first time only four years later in June 2006. The third proposal from the Daewoo Conference was the least contentious — building technical capacities for measuring dioxin in the soil at the Da Nang Airport. This work got underway in 2004 and proved to be a productive collaboration among the United States Environmental Protection Agency, VAST and the Vietnamese Ministry of Defense.

If a Vietnam-U.S. joint study of the impact of dioxin exposure on humans was not possible, there was another way forward, however — a Vietnam-Canada joint study of the levels of dioxin remaining in the soil from the wartime use of Agent Orange. The study would expand on the work that the Vietnam Ministry of Health's 10-80 Committee and Hatfield Consultants of Vancouver, Canada, carried out in 1994-99 to measure the impact of intensive spraying of Agent Orange in Aluoi District, a remote valley in central Vietnam.[20] The 10-80/Hatfield work in Aluoi was the first comprehensive long-term study of residual dioxin in Vietnam to be published in an international peer-reviewed scientific journal.[21] Their path-breaking work formed the basis for the dioxin hot spot hypothesis, an evidence-based concept that would focus the attention of the United States and Vietnam on the existence and status of residual dioxin at former American military bases in Vietnam.

In the early 2000s, the hot spot hypothesis offered the best way available to move forward on Agent Orange. It was scientific in nature, technical in execution and free of emotion and controversy. Testing samples of soil and pond sediments as well as fish, blood and breast milk, in Canada and publishing the findings in a peer-reviewed international scientific journal gave both visibility and credibility in the international scientific community and made the results harder to ignore. Hot-spot studies done in this way could replace ignorance and fear with knowledge and action, and, most importantly, draw in the United States Government.

In the spring of 2002, Charles Bailey wrote to Dr. Tran Manh Hung, the new director of the 10-80 Committee, saying, "We would like to invite the 10-80 Committee to prepare a formal proposal for possible Ford Foundation support. . . . We would provide the grant directly to the 10-80 Committee, who would be responsible for the management of all grant funds. . . . We view the proposed grant as an opportunity to produce a prioritized list of 'hot spots.' "[22] In response, the 10-80 Committee requested grant funding to establish a preliminary list of potentially dioxin-contaminated sites through a thorough search of records in Vietnam and American military archives; present a workshop open to all stakeholders to set the criteria for prioritizing the list, giving particular attention to the potential risks to children and pregnant women; collect and test samples of soils and pond sediments from each of the prioritized locations for the presence of dioxin; highlight those sites where further testing was required and warranted; and recommend strategies that could be immediately put in place to minimize or totally shield high-risk groups from exposure to contaminated soils. On September 5, 2002, the Ford Foundation approved a grant of $243,000 to the committee for this project.[23] Dr. Tran Manh Hung and his colleagues on the committee; Thomas Boivin, president; and Dr. Wayne Dwernychuk, senior scientist at Hatfield Consultants, got down to work. The search for the dioxin hot spots in Vietnam would take three years.

In June 2003, the United States deputy secretary of state, Richard Armitage, met the Vietnamese foreign affairs minister, Nguyen Dinh Bin, and acknowledged Vietnam's proposal for American assistance with dioxin remediation in Vietnam. In April 2004, Lewis M. Stern wrote to Senior Colonel Nguyen Ngoc Giao, military attaché of Vietnam in the United States. Stern reminded Giao that in 1995 the United States and Vietnam settled all government and private claims related to the war and agreed that the United States would not be responsible for damages alleged to have been related to Agent Orange. He added that American law barred the Defense Department from participating in the dioxin cleanup. The Defense Department could, however, give Vietnam access to records from the spraying program, provide information on remediation technologies and share the department's experience with managing dioxin contamination in the United States.[24]

Thus by 2003–2004, officials in the two governments were talking with each other about Agent Orange, but these talks intersected only in a limited way — the Vietnamese side continuing to request help across the board and the American side responding just with technical assistance for dioxin measurement (from the Environmental Protection Agency) and assurances of archival information on Operation Ranch Hand (Department of Defense). Early in 2003, Le Van Bang, then vice minister of foreign affairs, felt progress was slowing in the overall bilateral relationship. He proposed a conference in Washington on the future of the bilateral relationship and asked the Ford Foundation to fund it. The conference was structured to include not only officials from both countries but also Vietnamese Americans and leaders from business, nongovernmental organizations and universities. The topics would range from trade and investment to war legacies, including Agent Orange. The conference presaged two elements that would contribute importantly later in the decade to continued progress on Agent Orange — the bringing in of third parties, particularly NGOs, to the bilateral discussions on Agent Orange and recognition that the United States would need to come to terms with this war legacy in order to secure a sound long-term relationship with Vietnam.

Differing attitudes between the two countries continued to be evident in early 2006. A local leader in Aluoi District observed, "I don't care who did it, but whoever did that, I don't know from what country, but they should help the people in their lives."[25] VAVA said in its public appeal in March that "victims of Agent Orange/dioxin and their families are among the poorest and most unhappy of the society. Many thousands of victims have died without justice for themselves and their families."[26] Dr. Le Ke Son, director of the Office of Committee 33 and a government spokesman, commented, "The term 'toxic chemicals' or 'chemical war' have been ignored in front of public and courts. They only accept that they used herbicides and defoliants as they used to do in other places. The term 'toxic chemicals' and 'chemical war' are considered to be 'sensitive' because chemical companies who produced these substances are involved in [it]."[27] And the American ambassador to Vietnam, Michael W. Marine, observed, "Both sides have not handled this well . . . we are locked into positions. The U.S. has a moral, but perhaps not a legal, responsibility."[28]

Nevertheless, 2006 proved to be a turning point on the vexing question of Agent Orange. On the official American side, Ambassador Michael W. Marine and U.S. Senate staffer Tim Rieser played the leading roles in bringing about this sea change.

In February the 10-80 Committee and Hatfield presented the results of their three-year survey to locate all potential dioxin hot spots and quantify their possible toxicity. These results strengthened Vietnamese determination to address the issue head-on with the United States. For its part, the findings gave the United States the first specific and comprehensive information on the extent of the environmental challenge of residual Agent Orange and what might be required to remediate it. The United States Embassy added a new position of environment, science, technology and health officer[29] and brought in a Vietnamese-speaking expert from the Environmental Protection Agency[30] to establish regular working relationships with the technical staff of the Ministry of Defense.

The Joint Advisory Committee (JAC) held its first meeting in June 2006.[31] However, as the minutes noted, "Several areas were highlighted as further needs, including, for example, financial support for cleaning up of hot spots, humanitarian assistance and rehabilitation of individuals affected by Agent Orange/dioxin. These were deemed to be outside of the scope of the Joint Advisory Committee activities but are noted here for the record."[32] This tension between a broader consideration of what the U.S. side called "policy issues" and a narrower focus on just technical advice and sharing of information continued throughout the eight years of the JAC. On the other hand, the annual JAC meetings were something new — an innovation in how the United States and Vietnam approached each other on Agent Orange. The JAC became a forum to regularly assess the progress the two countries were making together. It engaged senior officials on both sides with those charged with leading the cleanup at the Da Nang Airport (technical staffs of Committee 33, Ministry of Defense and contractors), other countries assisting with cleanup (the Czech Republic and New Zealand), NGO leaders with projects assisting Vietnamese with disabilities and other donors (Ford Foundation). American ambassadors, beginning with Michael W. Marine, and the Vietnamese vice ministers of natural resources and environment opened each meeting, and the meeting closed with a press conference. It became the norm that all issues related to Agent Orange/ dioxin could be raised and discussed at the JAC, although this did not mean that actions would follow, particularly on issues of the impact of dioxin on the Vietnamese.

Looking back from the vantage of 2015, Marine recalled that when he arrived in Hanoi in September 2004:

> I wanted to know why we hadn't made more progress on the Agent Orange issue. In my view, one of the reasons was that there was a lack of commitment to actually addressing Agent Orange on the U.S. side. Just about everyone on the [embassy] staff . . . considered it a real problem. If we tried to address [it] we would end up in a situation that we couldn't manage or control. It wouldn't come out well. . . . The basic attitude I found in my discussions with American officials from various departments was that this was an issue they didn't really want to deal with, they didn't want to touch, because it was too hard. While no one actually told me to leave it alone, the basic attitude was this is not something you want to spend your time on.
>
> The more I looked at the issue and the more I talked with Vietnamese officials and others about it — Charles Bailey was very instrumental in motivating me to do more on this — I decided I wasn't going to accept the status quo and that we would try to do better on the issue. . . . So my approach was, let's focus on getting things done that are positive and a group effort between the two sides. . . . There [also] needed to be a change in the some of the

terminology and language that was used publicly on the issue. If you want the American people, and their representatives, the Congress, to approach and deal with this issue, you can't continue to hit them over the head. You have to find a way to make it seem to them the right thing to do and a positive step in the right direction.[33]

Additional events in 2006 prepared the ground for future progress on Agent Orange. The Ford Foundation stepped up its grant making and Charles Bailey confirmed support for projects in Da Nang and Quang Ngai Provinces to demonstrate cost-effective ways to increase services to people with disabilities, a survey of people with disabilities in other heavily impacted areas, public health messages on safe food for people living around the Bien Hoa Airport, and sending Vietnamese scientists to the annual meeting of the International Symposium on Halogenated Persistent Organic Pollutants, held in 2006 in Oslo.[34] In September, the Ford Foundation granted $462,800 to the Office of Committee 33 for a detailed assessment of dioxin residue at the Da Nang Airport, evaluation of pathways dioxin might be spreading into residential areas around the airport and design of structures to block any further movement. The United States Embassy contributed $400,000[35] and the United States Environmental Protection Agency provided continuing technical assistance. As the status of dioxin at the Da Nang Airport became clearer, the foundation provided a further $789,800 for a concrete cap over the most highly contaminated areas and rainwater drainage and filtering systems. Committee 33 and the Ministry of Defense executed the project, and by January 2008 wartime dioxin was no longer a public health threat in Da Nang. The United States Embassy in Hanoi had mobilized what funds it could from State Department sources for the cleanup at Da Nang but clearly additional resources would be required, and they would need to come from elsewhere within the United States Government. By chance, Vietnam was hosting the annual meeting of the leaders of the Asia Pacific Economic Consortium (APEC) in November, which brought President George W. Bush to Hanoi.

The American press and the United States Congress heightened their attention to Vietnam and the state of the bilateral relationship. A front page article in the *Washington Post* ten days before the Bush visit reported how Agent Orange/dioxin continued to impact Vietnamese and that the United States was planning a cleanup of the Da Nang Airport.[36] While President Bush was in Hanoi for the APEC meeting, he and Vietnamese President Nguyen Minh Triet officially recognized, for the first time at the highest level, the need to address the Agent Orange legacy.

Their joint statement included this:

> President Triet also expressed appreciation for the U.S. Government's increasing development assistance to Vietnam and urged the U.S. side to increase humanitarian assistance including through co-operation on areas such as unexploded ordnance and continued assistance to Vietnamese with disabilities.
>
> The United States and Vietnam also agreed that further joint efforts to address the environmental contamination near former dioxin storage sites would make a valuable contribution to the continued development of their bilateral relationship.[37]

Despite this statement, the Bush Administration (and later the Obama Administration) declined to request funds for Agent Orange in Vietnam in the president's budget. Any further U.S. government funding for Agent Orange activities in Vietnam would need to come through the initiative of Congress. In late December 2006, Tim Rieser, accompanied by Bobby Muller, the Vietnam veterans leader, went on a fact-finding mission to Hanoi. Rieser was foreign policy adviser to Senator Patrick Leahy and a professional staff member of the Senate Appropriations Subcommittee on State, Foreign Operations and Related Programs. Senator Leahy had a decades-long concern for war victims, and it has been Leahy, with assistance from Rieser, who has arranged for virtually all the subsequent American funding for Agent Orange in Vietnam.

The Ford Foundation was to bring other parties into the arena of Agent Orange — ultimately Vietnamese and American nongovernment organizations, United Nations agencies like UNICEF and the United Nations Development Program, international businesses like Hyatt Hotels and HSBC Bank, and other American foundations such as Rockefeller, Gates and Atlantic Philanthropies. Still, in 2006 at the end of an initial round of grant-making, Bailey felt the situation required an organization to directly target and break the logjam of enmity and shortsightedness — a genuinely two-way channel for heartfelt, humanitarian discourse between the two countries about this terrible tragedy. Bailey therefore proposed a high level citizen-to-citizen group to help break the logjam. The U.S.-Vietnam Dialogue Group on Agent Orange/Dioxin got underway in February 2007 with Ambassador Ton Nu Thi Ninh, vice chair of the Foreign Affairs Committee of Vietnam's National Assembly, and Walter Isaacson, president of the Aspen Institute in Washington, as the Vietnamese and American co-chairs. Susan V. Berresford, by then the president of the Ford Foundation, agreed to serve as Dialogue Group convener.[38] In its first meeting the members unanimously agreed that "Agent Orange is a humanitarian concern we can do something about." They set priorities for the two governments and publicized them: expand service to people with disabilities, restore damaged landscapes, eliminate dioxin in Da Nang, raise funds for a high-resolution dioxin testing laboratory and educate key publics in the United States. The Dialogue Group members together visited officials on both sides seeking common ground and checking on progress. In 2010, the group published the first comprehensive plan for addressing all aspects of the Agent Orange legacy over a ten-year period.[39] The plan became a focal point for discussions on Agent Orange and was reinforced by subsequent Dialogue Group annual reports.[40]

In late March 2007, Dr. Le Ke Son, together with Major General Nguyen Ngoc Duong, director of the Department of Science, Technology and Environment at the Ministry of Defense, led a delegation to the United States to lock in these gains at meetings with the Senate Appropriations Subcommittee on the State, Foreign Operations and Related Programs; the Environmental Protection Agency; the United Nations Development Program/Global Environment Fund and the Ford Foundation. In May 2007, Congress approved the first $3 million toward work on Agent Orange in Vietnam. The sum was small so as not to attract attention[41] and the Appropriations Committee report accompanying the appropriation did not mention Agent Orange.

The report said: "Vietnam — The Committee recommends $3,000,000 to continue training of Vietnamese officials on environmental remediation techniques, for an initial contribution to the development of a national plan for such remediation, and for pilot programs for the remediation of Vietnam conflict-era chemical storage sites, and to address the health needs of nearby communities. The Committee requests the State

Department to consult with the Committee in a timely manner on the proposed uses of these funds."[42]

In July, Ambassador Michael W. Marine became the first senior American official to visit the dioxin-contaminated area of the Da Nang Airport. It would, however, take the State Department fifteen months more to assign the Agency for International Development to the tasks listed in the appropriation and for the work to begin. In consequence, Congress appropriated no further funds for Agent Orange in 2008 until the initial allocation could be spent. USAID funded three American NGOs to augment disability services in Da Nang "regardless of cause" in three-year projects, which began in October 2008. In 2011, it refocused its disability assistance on one American contractor, DAI, for work principally in Da Nang, with some assistance to the other dioxin hot spot locales, Bien Hoa and Phu Cat. In 2015, the aid agency replaced this with a third approach – a program of grants with awards going directly to Vietnamese and American NGOs for a wide variety of disability projects. By this time, however, the Congress had become more specific and appropriated funds as a humanitarian response to the specific legacy of Agent Orange.

As for the Da Nang Airport, following environmental impact assessments of the proposed cleanup, in September 2010, Ambassador Michael W. Michalak wrote to the deputy minister of defense, Senior Lieutenant General Nguyen Huy Hieu, to propose a project that would start in 2011 and be completed in 2013.[43] The cost was initially estimated at $42 million from the United States and counterpart funding of $1.7 million from Vietnam. However, further technical complexities occurred. Ambassador David B. Shear and Lieutenant General Nguyen Chi Vinh, deputy minister of defense, officially opened the project on August 9, 2012. Since then the volume of soils and pond sediments requiring treatment has proved to be higher than the initial estimate with the result that the project is now expected to be completed in 2018 at a cost of $108 million: $105 million from the U.S. and $3 million from the Vietnamese Ministry of Defense for clearance of unexploded ordnance, a power substation and project management.[44]

Congressional appropriations from 2009 onward fueled the American partnership with Vietnam to address the legacies of Agent Orange.

As experience and knowledge on the American side improved, the annual allocations increased, and the accompanying language guiding their use became more specific. Charles Bailey's comparative study of Agent Orange victims and other Vietnamese with disabilities proposed a way to focus United States assistance on those believed to be impacted by dioxin.[45] By 2016 the annual appropriations act read:

> Vietnam — (1) Dioxin remediation — Funds appropriated by this Act under the heading "Economic Support Fund" shall be made available for remediation of dioxin contaminated sites in Vietnam and may be made available for assistance for the Government of Vietnam, including the military, for such purposes. (2) Health and disability programs — Funds appropriated by this Act under the heading "Development Assistance" shall be made available for health and disability programs in areas sprayed with Agent Orange and otherwise contaminated with dioxin, to assist individuals with severe upper or lower body mobility impairment and/or cognitive or developmental disabilities."[46]

This language has continued to be used in subsequent appropriations acts.

In early 2016 the American Academy of Motion Picture Arts and Sciences nominated *Chau, Beyond the Lines* for an Oscar.[47] The film, directed by Courtney Marsh, is about Le Minh Chau, a teenager growing up in Ho Chi Minh City with disabilities linked to his mother's exposure to Agent Orange. The film follows Chau over seven years as he struggles with the reality of his dream to become a professional artist. Although *Chau* did not win the Oscar, it is a well-told and compelling story and has helped bring the U.S. and Vietnam closer. In March 2016, Ambassador Ted Osius screened it at the American Centers in Hanoi and Ho Chi Minh City. In June of the same year, under the initiative of Vietnam's permanent representative to the United Nations, Ambassador Nguyen Phuong Nga, the U.S. and Vietnam sponsored a showing of the film in New York at the annual meeting on the U.N. Convention on the Rights of People with Disabilities. A year later, *Chau* was screened on Capitol Hill with the sponsorship of Senator Patrick J. Leahy.

President Barack Obama visited Vietnam in 2016, nine years after the first joint statement of the two countries on the dioxin war legacy. This time the joint statement read:

> Both countries expressed their satisfaction with their joint effort to advance humanitarian and war legacy issues. . . . Vietnam welcomed cooperation leading to the successful conclusion of the first phase of dioxin remediation at Da Nang International Airport, with the final phase already underway. The United States committed to partnering with Vietnam to make a significant contribution to the cleanup of dioxin contamination at Bien Hoa Air Base."[48]

President Obama added, in a speech at the International Center in Hanoi, "Even as we continue to assist Vietnamese with disabilities, including children, we are also continuing to help remove Agent Orange-dioxin."[49] His words went beyond those in the joint statement to both mention Agent Orange and link it with disability and dioxin and a continuing American role in assisting Vietnam with both.

In May 2017, the Vietnamese secured a meeting between Prime Minister Nguyen Xuan Phuc and President Donald J. Trump. This set the scene for Trump's November visit to Da Nang for the 2017 APEC Heads of State meeting, followed by an official visit to Vietnam.[50] The Vietnamese sought a reaffirmation of the commitment the previous American administration had made to a "significant contribution to the cleanup of dioxin contamination at Bien Hoa Air Base." The Trump Administration's response came in two parts: a press conference in Da Nang the day before the president arrived, and a joint statement following the presidential visit in Hanoi. The State Department's press release stated:

> In anticipation of President Donald J. Trump's visit to Vietnam, Under Secretary [Thomas A.] Shannon announced that the United States is committed to contribute to join U.S.-Vietnam dioxin remediation efforts at the Bien Hoa Air Base. A 2016 U.S.-Vietnam joint environmental assessment found that the volume of dioxin contamination at Bien Hoa Airbase makes it the largest dioxin hotspot in Vietnam, highlighting the significance of this next area of cooperation.[51]

In paragraph 7 of the joint statement, the two presidents had this to say about war legacies.

> Both leaders reaffirmed the importance of continued cooperation to address the legacies of war. In this regard, President Tran Dai Quang expressed appreciation for the United States' contribution to the successful dioxin remediation at Da Nang Airport and welcomed the United States' commitment to contribute to remediation at Bien Hoa Airport. He welcomed further U.S. assistance for persons with disabilities. President Trump expressed his appreciation for Vietnam's full and continued cooperation in accounting for U.S. personnel still missing from the war, and pledged to cooperate with Viet Nam in its efforts to locate its missing soldiers. The two leaders committed to cooperation in the removal of explosive remnants of war.[52]

This is the first joint statement ever to juxtapose dioxin remediation at an airport hot spot and assistance for persons with disabilities under the heading of war legacies. The joint statement language confirms how over the years the Agent Orange effort has grown into a program that both governments fully acknowledge and indeed point to as an example of how the two countries are trying to address one of the unfortunate consequences of the war. However, as of the end of 2017, the question facing the United States is whether the Pentagon will partner with the State Department to provide the additional funds needed for a meaningful contribution to the Bien Hoa cleanup. At the same time, USAID needs to continue its high-impact programs assisting Vietnamese with severe disabilities in the areas that were heavily sprayed.

The Future of
Agent Orange

It is easy to forget how insoluble the problem of Agent Orange/ dioxin seemed not so long ago. At first, the Agent Orange/dioxin issue was highly controversial and "off limits," as our two nations cautiously began to explore their post-war relationship. When it became a topic of tentative discussion, the problem still seemed insoluble. It appeared to be too large, affecting too many places and people, and it lacked scientific certainty about causality and cure. The first breakthrough on Agent Orange was the dioxin-hot-spot hypothesis — when both sides agreed to focus cleanup on three dangerously contaminated dioxin hot spots. The second breakthrough was evidence that a large majority of Agent Orange victims were among the severely disabled.

Today, we can be proud that our countries have, in varying ways, solved these puzzles that seemed so difficult just a few years ago. Vietnam launched monthly payments to help hundreds of thousands of Agent Orange victims. It also isolated the worst of the dioxin-contaminated soils at Bien Hoa and brought in the UNDP/Global Environmental Facility to assist with placing the dioxin residues at Phu Cat in a secure landfill, and the Ford Foundation to begin the cleanup of dioxin at Da Nang. Since 2007, the U.S. Congress has appropriated $231.2 million to address Agent Orange in Vietnam — three-quarters of it to clean up the dioxin at the Da Nang Airport and one-quarter benefiting Vietnamese with disabilities. The Da Nang Airport is now free of dioxin, and tens of thousands of Vietnamese with disabilities have received help. Most importantly, the two governments now have a practical partnership. The extreme sensitivity of this subject is a thing of the past.

But much remains to be done. Phu Cat and Da Nang held only 15 percent of the soil requiring remediation. The remaining 85 percent — some 495,300 cubic meters or 750,000 U.S. tons — is at the Bien Hoa Airbase, 20 miles upstream of Ho Chi Minh City's 8.5 million people. USAID estimates that remediation there will cost at least $395 million and take a decade. The Vietnamese Ministry of Defense estimates $500 million. In addition, several hundred thousand young Vietnamese still await help in coping with disabilities linked to dioxin exposure of a parent or grandparent (or even a great-grandparent).

Trust and cooperation between former enemies are often rebuilt and fortified through the work the parties do to remediate the terrible aftermath of war. Postwar measures will never be able to erase deep scars, restore personal losses or make up for great hardship. However, if they are undertaken in good spirit and with vigor and sincerity, they can unite people on a forward path of mutual respect and friendship. Both Vietnam and the United States want to move forward in this way together.

The end of the disaster of Agent Orange/dioxin is within the reach of people of goodwill on both sides — both those in government and in civilian life. This end will be achieved through joint effort, compromise and agreement on solutions and end points. Given the positive record of collaboration and partnership since 2007, it would be foolish, and indeed disgraceful, not to carry through to the completion of the task.

Some commentators on the U.S. side ask: When will it be done? Given the size and the complexity of the Agent Orange/dioxin legacy and the Vietnamese concern about it, it is an understandable question. There is no simple answer, nor one that will satisfy each and every person. The best solution is to figure out now what a vigorous and substantial commitment would be that could dramatically alter the life circumstances of many affected individuals and families. If that sum is properly expended and the partnership remains strong, perhaps the end will then be achieved or in sight. The Bien Hoa Air Base cleanup will take at least a decade, and U.S. health/disabilities assistance should continue during that time. It is very difficult to estimate the costs. But if the U.S. spends a minimum of $50 million each year for the next ten years — divided between Bien Hoa and health/disabilities assistance — significant progress will be made.

We have no doubt that the Vietnamese will keep pressure on their officials to continue. But American citizens who are guided by the moral pillars of curiosity, empathy and reciprocity have a responsibility here as well. Americans in large numbers need to tell their senators and representatives, "We're proud of what our government has achieved in Vietnam. Now is the time to double down and finish the job. Help the Vietnamese struggling with severe disabilities. Clean up the dioxin we left at the Bien Hoa Air Base in Vietnam."

We humbly ask you to look no further than our collaboration as authors on this book for a model of how Americans and Vietnamese can successfully find common ground, agree on evidence and jointly propose what needs to be done to bring to an end, to the fullest extent possible, the terrible legacy of Agent Orange. We hope others will find this book a useful tool to that end.

ACKNOWLEDGMENTS

S on's family encouraged and helped him a lot in researching and overcoming the consequences of Agent Orange as well as with the writing of this book. To his wife, Thai Thi Hoa, and sons Le Tuan Anh and Le Thai Anh, many thanks! For years Charles's family has listened to his stories, put up with his absences, and encouraged him onward as he followed the twists and turns of Agent Orange. To his wife, Ingrid Foik, and daughters Eliza Bailey and Sabine Bailey — many, many thanks for your steadfast support!

We want to recognize and thank Susan V. Berresford of the Ford Foundation. In 1993 Susan witnessed the terrible legacy of Agent Orange firsthand when she visited Vietnam to explore opening a Ford Foundation office in Hanoi. She didn't forget it. Shortly after she became the Ford Foundation president in 1996, the foundation opened its Hanoi office, and she sent Charles Bailey to Hanoi to head it. Over the next decade she approved Ford grants and advocacy on Agent Orange, including grants that Le Ke Son used to begin the cleanup of dioxin at the Da Nang airport. In 2007 Susan convened the U.S.-Vietnam Dialogue Group on Agent Orange/Dioxin and she has continued to be a source of ideas and encouragement right down to the present.

We also warmly thank Ngo Le Mai, another leader at the Ford Foundation. Le Mai was grants administrator in the Hanoi office 1997–2009. Her ability to build sound and productive relationships around this often sensitive subject and her sure sense of what to do next went far beyond just getting the grants made. She also was key to the writing of this book, translating back and forth over many hours and helping us understand each other better than we might have otherwise.

Beginning in 2000 and continuing for over a decade, the Ford Foundation funded Vietnamese and Americans to develop the facts necessary for constructive dialogue on Agent Orange, explore and demonstrate practical solutions, experience success together and develop a common understanding of the way forward. The foundation approved seventy-eight grants to organizations that totaled $17.1 million for these purposes. We thank the foundation for its early, steady and unfailing support for this work, particularly Katherine Fuller and then Irene Hirano, the chairs of the Ford Foundation's Board of Trustees during this time, and Alison Bernstein and then Pablo Farias, the vice presidents with oversight of the Vietnam program. We thank Darren Walker, the foundation's current president, for his warm encouragement and help.

The staff of Le Ke Son's Office of Committee 33 made available information that enabled us to present a comprehensive picture of the Agent Orange legacy in this book. We thank them and particularly the deputy director of the office, Dr. Nguyen My Hang, and Dr. Nguyen Hung Minh, head of the Dioxin and Toxic Chemicals Laboratory in the Vietnam Environment Administration. They have contributed greatly to overcoming the consequences of Agent Orange/dioxin.

During the writing of this book we formally interviewed thirty-seven people and consulted with many others. We thank each of you for helping us to better understand your perspective on this complex subject. Any errors of fact or interpretation are of course our own.

Bui The Giang, *External Relations Commission of the Communist Party of Vietnam*

Do Hung Viet, *Ministry of Foreign Affairs*

Ambassador Ha Huy Thong, *Foreign Affairs Committee, National Assembly of Vietnam*

Le Van Bang, *Vietnam Ministry of Foreign Affairs*

Luong Thi Huong, *Children of Vietnam*

Ambassador Ngo Quang Xuan, *Foreign Affairs Committee, National Assembly of Vietnam*

Ambassador Nguyen Phuong Nga, *Permanent Representative of S. R. Vietnam to the United Nations*

Nguyen Thanh Tuan, *photographer*

Nguyen Thi Hien, *Vietnam Association of Victims of Agent Orange/ Da Nang*

Dr. Nguyen Thi Ngoc Phuong, *Medical University of Ho Chi Minh City*

Senior Lieutenant General Nguyen Van Rinh, *Vietnam Association of Victims of Agent Orange*

Nguyen Viet Cuong, *National Economics University*

Ambassador Ton Nu Thi Ninh, *Foreign Affairs Committee, National Assembly of Vietnam*

Ambassador Pham Quang Vinh, *Vietnamese Ambassador to the U.S. 2015–*

Colonel Tran Ngoc Tam, *Vietnam Association of Victims of Agent Orange*

Truong Van Thom, *Children of Vietnam*

Vo Duc Dam, *deputy prime minister of Vietnam*

Professor Vo Quy, *Vietnam Center for Natural Resources and Environmental Studies*

Vu Khoan, *former deputy prime minister of Vietnam*

Vu Xuan Hong, *Vietnam Union of Friendship Organizations*

Christopher Abrams, *USAID/Hanoi*

Thomas G. Boivin, *Hatfield Consultants, Ltd.*

James Bond, *Bond & Associates*

Patrick Brady, *Bond & Associates*

Sally Benson, *Chino Cienega Foundation*

Kathy Bonk, *Communications Consortium Media Center*

Frederick Z. Brown, *Paul H. Nitze School of Advanced International Studies*

Raymond Burghardt, *U. S. Ambassador to Vietnam 2001–2004*

David Devlin-Foltz, *Aspen Institute*

Michael DiGregorio, *The Asia Foundation*

Gay Dillingham, *CNS Communications*

Wayne Dwernychuk, *Hatfield Consultants, Ltd.*

William Farland, *U.S. Environmental Protection Agency*

Kenneth Feinberg, *attorney, Feinberg Rozen*

Vance Fong, *U.S. Environmental Protection Agency*

Virginia Foote, U.S.-Vietnam Trade Council

Jerry Frank, producer, *Chau, Beyond the Lines*

Jon Funabiki, *San Francisco State University*

Elliot Gerson, *Aspen Institute*

Thao Griffiths, *Vietnam Veterans of America Foundation*

Michael Greene, *USAID/Hanoi*

Susan Hammond, *War Legacies Project*

Christopher Harris, *Consultant*

Chris Hatfield, *Hatfield Consultants, Ltd.*

Andrew Herrup, *U.S. Department of State*

Murray Hiebert, *Center for Strategic and International Studies*

Donna Horney, *Aspen Institute*

David Hulse, *Ford Foundation*

Walter Isaacson, *Aspen Institute*

Wilmot James, *Columbia University*

Janice Joseph, *Aspen Institute*

Catherine Karnow, *photographer*

Dean Kokkoris, *Bureau of Labor Law, New York City*

Nga Le, *entrepreneur*

Dr. Thu Le, *University of Virginia*

Senator Patrick J. Leahy, *United States Senate*

Nancy Letteri, *Children of Vietnam*

Michael W. Marine, *U.S. Ambassador to Vietnam 2004–2007*

Courtney Marsh, *director,* Chau, Beyond the Lines

Michael F. Martin, *Congressional Research Service,*
Library of Congress

Edwin Martini, *Western Michigan University*

Daniel Mont, *Center for Inclusive Policy*

Bobby Muller, *Veterans for America*

Steve Nichols, *Chino Cienega Foundation*

Joanne Omang, *Communications Consortium Media Center*

Douglas S. O'Neill, *U.S. Department of State*

Charles Ornstein, *Propublica*

Ted Osius, *U.S. Ambassador to Vietnam 2014–2017*

Joakim Parker, *USAID/Hanoi*

Thomas Bo Pedersen, *Mascot International/Vietnam*

Son Michael Pham, *Kids Without Borders*

Tim Rieser, *U.S. Senate Committee on Appropriations*

Nathan Sage, *U.S. Department of State*

Anne P. Sassaman, *National Institute of Environmental Health Sciences*

Chuck Searcy, *Project RENEW*

Kenneth Sharpe, *Swarthmore College*

Robert Schiffer, *U.S.-Vietnam Trade Council*

Richard and Dabney Schmitt, *Landon Carter Schmitt Memorial Fund*

Pat Schroeder, *former Member of Congress*

Phil Sparks, *Communication Consortium Media Center*

Lee A. Smithey, *Swarthmore College*

Jeanne M. Stellman, *Columbia University*

Kevin Teichman, *U.S. Environmental Protection Agency*

Karen Tramontano, *Blue Star Strategies*

Ca Van Tran, *Vietnam Assistance for the Handicapped (VNAH)*

Diep Vuong, *Pacific Links Foundation*

Rick Weidman, *Vietnam Veterans of America*

Christie Todd Whitman, *Whitman Strategy Group*

William Wise, *Paul H. Nitze School of Advanced International Studies*

Linda Yarr, *George Washington University*

Peter Zinoman, *University of California/ Berkeley*

James G. Zumwalt, *U.S. Marine Corps*

Mary Zurbuchen, *International Fellowship Program*

G. A. Beller, Managing Principal at G. Anton Companies in Chicago, stepped in at a critical moment to deftly steer us through the publication process. G. Anton Publishing General Manager Vivian Craig made it look easy, with her sound advice, swift execution, and unfailing good cheer, and Editor Maya Meyers' attention to detail expertly polished the manuscript. We are greatly in their debt.

The American Council of Learned Societies (ACLS), New York, administered our book project. We thank ACLS vice president Steven Wheatley; Minh Kauffman, ACLS Center for Educational Exchange with Vietnam; Kelly Buttermore, grants administrator; Irv Molotsky, copy editor, and Nicole Buckley, production consultant. Grants to the ACLS covered the costs of travel, translation, writing and distribution of the book. We deeply appreciate the support of the Chino Cienega Foundation (Palm Springs, California), the Ford Foundation (New York), the Kaiser Family Foundation (Menlo Park, California), the Mott Foundation (Flint, Michigan), the Passport Foundation (San Francisco) and an individual donor.

What Is Dioxin?

Dioxin is a general term that describes a group of organic compounds that are highly persistent in the environment. It forms a colorless crystalline solid with no distinguishable odor at room temperature. Dioxin is nearly insoluble in water and tends to be strongly absorbed onto the surfaces of soil particles. It is stable against heat, acids and alkali but it will decompose when exposed to sunlight.[1]

Dioxins are persistent organic pollutants (POPs), so named because they take a long time to break down once they are in the environment. They accumulate in and are biomagnified up the food chain, particularly in the fatty tissues of animals. Dioxins are highly toxic. Over 90 percent of human exposure to dioxins is through food, mainly meat, dairy products, fish and shellfish.

Research in the 1970s and 1980s showed that dioxin can cause cancer,[2] reproductive and developmental problems,[3] and damage the immune system[4] in monkeys, rats and guinea pigs.

Dioxins are the unintentional byproducts of combustion and metallurgical processes, the manufacturing of chemicals, improper incineration of municipal solid waste and medical waste, coal-fired power plants, forest fires and residential burning of wood and household plastics. In the 1970s and 1980s, dioxin was found in buried chemical wastes at Love Canal in Niagara Falls, New York, and in the 1980s in waste oil from electrical transformers used to control dust on country roads in Times Beach, Missouri. In 1976, an accident at a chemical plant in Seveso, Italy, released dioxin into the air. These and other instances of dioxin in the environment led to serious illnesses and health complications among those who had been exposed.

Toxic equivalents, or TEQs, are used to report the toxicity-weighted masses of mixtures of dioxins. The TEQ method of dioxin reporting is more meaningful than simply reporting the total number of grams of a mixture of variously toxic compounds because some dioxins are more toxic than others. Dioxin concentrations are reported in either parts per trillion (ppt) TEQ or in picograms per gram (pg/g) TEQ, one picogram being one trillionth of a gram. These are equivalent measurements.

The most toxic of the dioxin compounds is 2,3,7,8-tetrachlorodibenzo-p-dioxin, or TCDD. The toxicity of other dioxins and chemicals like polychlorinated dibenzodioxins (PCBs) that act like dioxin are measured in relation to TCDD. When 2,3,7,8 TCDD accounts for 80 to 100 percent of the TEQ, it is presumptive evidence that the dioxin originated in Agent Orange or one of the other herbicides used by the United States during the Vietnam War.

To calculate TEQ, each dioxin compound is assigned a toxic equivalency factor, or TEF, as in the table opposite. This factor denotes a given dioxin compound's toxicity relative to 2,3,7,8-TCDD, which is assigned the maximum toxicity designation of 1. To obtain the TEQ of a dioxin mixture, one simply multiplies the concentration of each compound in the mixture by its TEF and then totals them.

Dioxins	Toxic Equivalency Factor (TEF)
2,3,7,8-TCDD	1.0
1,2,3,7,8-PnCDD	1.0
1,2,3,4,7,8-HxCDD	0.1
1,2,3,6,7,8-HxCDD	0.1
1,2,3,7,8,9-HxCDD	0.1
1,2,3,4,6,7,8-HpCDD	0.01
OCDD	0.0001
2,3,7,8-TCDF	0.1
1,2,3,7,8-PnCDF	0.05
2,3,4,7,8-PnCDF	0.5
1,2,3,4,7,8-HxCDF	0.1
1,2,3,6,7,8-HxCDF	0.1
1,2,3,7,8,9-HxCDF	0.1
2,3,4,6,7,8-HxCDF	0.1
1,2,3,4,6,7,8-HpCDF	0.01
1,2,3,4,7,8,9-HpCDF	0.01
OCDF	0.0001

Government of Vietnam Recent Scientific Research on Agent Orange/Dioxin 2011–2015

In November 2011, the Vietnamese minister of science and technology appointed Dr. Le Ke Son to manage the next round of scientific research on Agent Orange/dioxin. The program comprised twelve subjects, ran from 2011 to 2015, and cost VND 77,490 million ($3.7 million). The program has published these scientific papers.

N. H. Minh, N. V. Thuong, V. D. Nam, L. K. Son, N. V. Thuy, H. D. Tung, N. A. Tuan, T. B. Minh, D. Q. Huy, The Emission of Polychlorinated Dibenzo-p-dioxins and Polychlorinated Dibenzofurans from Steel and Cement-Kiln Plants in Vietnam. *Aerosol and Air Quality Research*, Vol. 14: 1189–1198; 2014.

———, Determination of PCDD/Fs in breast milk of women living in the vicinity of Da Nang Agent Orange hotspot (Vietnam) and estimation of the infant's daily intake. *Science of the Total Environment*, Vol. 491-492: pp. 212-218; 2014.

————, Transport and bioaccumulation of Polychlorinated dibenzo-p-dioxins and polychlorinated dibenzo-furans at the Bien Hoa Agent Orange Hotspot, Vietnam, *Environmental Science and Pollution Research*, Vol. 22, pp. 14431-14441; 2015.

V. L. Anh, H. K. Hue, P. V. Duc, Proposed integrated technology to thoroughly treat Agent Orange/Dioxin in soil and sediment, *Journal of Catalysis and Adsorption*, No. 4, 2015.

V. C. Thang, P. L. Anh, V. T. Son, D. T. Tuyen, Dioxin content in human blood after 1972 (U.S. military ended spraying of Agent Orange/dioxin), *Journal of Practical Medicine*, Issue 10, Hanoi, 2015.

————, Dioxin content in fish samples in regions of Vietnam, *Journal of Toxicology*, Vol. 32, Hanoi, 2016.

T. V. Khoa, N. D. Bac, D. T. Truong, N. V. Dieu, N. M. Tam , D. M. Trung, N. X. Truong, Study of the health dynamics of Agent Orange/dioxin victims through clinical examination. *Journal of Clinical Medicine* 108, Hanoi, 2015.

————, Study of the change of blood biochemical index on subjects with high levels of dioxin in blood. *Journal of Vietnamese Medicine*, No. 2, Hanoi, 2015.

T. D. Phan, T. Q. Dai, L. T. Lan Anh, P. T. Hoan, P. T. Phuong, Research and Application of Some Methods to Prenatal Diagnosis and Genetic Counseling for Avoiding Adverse Pregnancy Outcomes and Birth Defects, *Proceedings* of the Scientific Program on "Research on the Consequences of Agent Orange/Dioxin used by the United States in the Vietnam War for Human and the Environment in Vietnam," Hanoi, 2016.

N. D. Ton, V. P. Nhung, N. H. Ha, P. N. Khoi, N. T. Duong, Research on Change of Gene and Chromosome in human with high level of dioxin in blood. *Proceedings* of the Scientific Program on "Research on the Consequences of Agent Orange/Dioxin used by the United States in the Vietnam War for Humans and the Environment in Vietnam," Hanoi, 2016.

N. H. Thanh, N. M. An, D. Quyet, N. B. Vuong, Evaluate the effect of treatment with nonspecific detoxification method for those exposed to dioxin. *Journal of Toxicology*, No. 30, Hanoi, 2015.

P. T. Tai, M. Nishijo, H. V. Luong, D. M. Trung, N. V. Long, N. T. Linh, P. V. Son, H. Nishijo, Dioxin concentrations in blood and food consumption habits of a population living near Bien Hoa Air Base, a hotspot of dioxin contamination in Vietnam. *Organohalogen Compounds, 2015, Vol. 77, 123-126.*

N. M. Phuong, N. T. Linh, H. C. Sa, Psychological trauma of Agent Orange victims in Bien Hoa city. *Journal of Vietnamese Medicine*, No. 2, Hanoi, 2015.

N. B. Vuong, N. L. Toan, H. A. Son, P. T. Hien Luong, Research on clinical characteristics, histopathological histories of liver parenchyma, some liver function tests in humans exposed to Agent Orange/dioxin. *Journal of Military Medicine,* 433, Hanoi, 2015.

———, Study of CYPIA1 genes in people exposed to Agent Orange/dioxin. *Journal of Practical Medicine,* No. 994, Hanoi, 2016.

P. V. Loi, B. H. Nam, N. T. Thu Hoai, N. H. Dung, T. V. Chau, Method of assessing the damage to forest resources used by Agent Orange/dioxin during the Vietnam War. *Journal of the Environment*, No. 11, Hanoi, 2015.

N. T. Luc, T. N. Tam, Research evaluation of the policy for Resistance Fighters and for other exposed people, *Proceedings* of the Scientific Program on "Research on the Consequences of Agent Orange/Dioxin used by the United States in the Vietnam War for Human and the Environment in Vietnam," Hanoi, 2016.

Ford Foundation Grant Recipients Agent Orange/Dioxin in Vietnam Program 2000–2011

TOTAL: Seventy-eight grants worth $17.1 million over twelve years

Goal: Assist Vietnamese with disabilities & reduce risks to public health (26 grants: $7,385,339)

Grant	Year	Description
Vietnam Red Cross, Agent Orange Victim's Fund	2000	Support for community-based rehabilitation programs for Vietnamese with disabilities to assist Vietnamese with disabilities in three provinces
Vietnam Public Health Association	2006	Education on food safety in neighborhoods surrounding the Bien Hoa Airbase
Vietnam Veterans of America Foundation (VVAF)	2006	Survey of healthcare needs of Vietnamese with disabilities in 11 provinces, assessment of local NGO services & assistance
Institute for Social Development Studies	2007	Field survey & National Conference on situation & needs of Vietnamese with disabilities
Thai Binh Red Cross	2007	Services for Vietnamese with disabilities & training for family members and health care providers in Thai Binh province
East Meets West Foundation	2007	Technical support to Thai Binh Red Cross & medical, educational & job training services for Vietnamese with disabilities in the province
East Meets West Foundation	2007	Collaboration with Da Nang Rehabilitation Center for surgery & prosthetic devices & education and job training for Vietnamese with disabilities in Quang Ngai province
Vietnam Veterans of America Foundation (VVAF)	2008	Upgrade services & organize self-help groups for Vietnamese with disabilities in Thai Binh, Ninh Dinh, Nam Dinh, Thua-Thien Hue, & Quang Nam provinces & Da Nang
Vietnam Assistance to the Handicapped (VNAH)	2008	Services for Vietnamese with disabilities and build overseas support
Disability Resource & Development (DRD)	2008	Services & small grant fund for self-help groups of Vietnamese with disabilities
Disability Resource & Development (DRD)	2008	Counseling, training, website & clubhouse for self-help groups of Vietnamese with disabilities
Institute for Social Development Studies	2008	Training of trainers for officially-supported program to counter stigma and discrimination against people with disabilities

Grant	Year	Description
U.S. Fund for UNICEF	2008	Matching fund to mobilize donors for UNICEF program on childhood disability in Vietnam
Hai Chau District Peoples Committee, Da Nang	2008	Implement the 'Hope System of Care,' case management-based individualized services for disabled children in the district
Children of Vietnam	2008	Technical support to Hai Chau District's 'Hope System of Care' for disabled children
Can Tho Association of People with Disabilities	2009	Increase jobs and incomes for Vietnamese with disabilities in Can Tho
Center for Social Work and Community Development (SRDC)	2009	Counseling & job training for Vietnamese with disabilities in Bien Hoa
Institute for Social Development Studies	2009	Raise awareness of rights of people with disabilities
Ngu Hanh Son District Peoples Committee, Da Nang	2009	Introduce the 'Hope System of Care,' case management-based individualized services for disabled children in the district
Children of Vietnam	2009	Technical support to Ngu Hanh Son District's 'Hope System of Care' for disabled children
Institute of International Education	2009	Travel awards for Vietnamese
Vietnam Public Health Association	2009	Public education on food safety in neighborhoods surrounding Da Nang airport
National Steering Committee 33	2010	National Seminar on birth defects and newborn screening before the 2010 meeting of the Joint Advisory Committee(JAC)
National Foundation for the Centers for Disease Control	2010	American scientists' participation in the National Seminar
National Steering Committee 33	2010	Follow up activities to the National Seminar
Vietnam Assistance for the Handicapped (VNAH)	2011	Expansion of pilot database on people with disabilities in Da Nang

Goal: Remediate dioxin-contaminated soils (16 grants: $2,680,300)

Grant	Year	Description
Ministry of Health, 10-80 Committee with Hatfield Consultants	2002	Identify & assess dioxin hot spots at all former American military bases in central and southern Vietnam
Institute of International Education	2006	Travel awards for Vietnamese scientists to present their research at the 26th International Symposium on Halogenated Persistent Organic Pollutants, Oslo
National Steering Committee 33 with Hatfield Consultants	2006	Analyze the current danger from the dioxin hot spot at the Da Nang Airport through the soil and food chain
National Steering Committee 33 with Hatfield Consultants	2006	Assess the flow characteristics of dioxin-contaminated soils away from the dioxin hot spot and analyze options for containment to prevent further spread of dioxin pending full remediation at the Da Nang Airport
National Steering Committee 33	2007	Lay concrete cap & filter drainage water to halt movement of dioxin into residential areas surrounding the Da Nang Airport & to stop contamination of the food chain
Vietnam National University/ Hanoi, Center for Natural Resources & Environmental Studies	2007	Train farmers, technicians & land managers to restore uplands degraded by Agent Orange in Quang Tri province
Institute of International Education	2007	Travel awards for Vietnamese scientists to present their research at the 27th International Symposium on Halogenated Persistent Organic Pollutants, Tokyo
Institute of International Education	2008	Travel awards for Vietnamese
National Steering Committee 33	2008	Analyze current levels of dioxin in soils, foodstuffs and people living near the Da Nang Airport following construction of measures to contain dioxin-contamination within the airport
Institute of International Education	2009	Travel awards for Vietnamese
National Steering Committee 33	2009	Test the effectiveness of a bioremediation technology for cleanup of dioxin-contaminated soil at Da Nang airport & provide logistical support for a U.S.-Vietnam environmental remediation task force

Ford Foundation Grant Recipients
Agent Orange/Dioxin in Vietnam Program 2000-2011

Grant	Year	Description
U.S. Environmental Protection Agency	2009	Scientific support for the bioremediation pilot treatment project at Da Nang Airport
U.S. Environmental Protection Agency	2010	Evaluation of bioremediation field test at Da Nang airport
SGS North America	2010	Laboratory analysis of field test of bioremediation of dioxin at Da Nang airport
National Steering Committee 33 with Hatfield Consultants	2010	Take samples and analyze current levels of dioxin in soils, foodstuffs and people living near the Bien Hoa Airbase
Vietnam National University/ Hanoi, Center for Natural Resources & Environmental Studies	2010	Train farmers, technicians and land managers to restore uplands degraded by Agent Orange in Thua-Thien Hue province

Goal: Educate the American people (37 grants: $7,067,501):

Grant	Year	Description
Diplomatic Academy of Vietnam	2003	Conference on "The Future of the US-Vietnam Relationship," Washington, D.C.
Aspen Institute	2007	Explore the possibility of a Track II process between the U.S. & Vietnam on Agent Orange
Aspen Institute	2007	Promote dialogue in the U.S. & between the US and Vietnam on Agent Orange
National Organization on Disability	2008	Survey the impact of Agent Orange on American veterans' health
Institute of International Education	2008	Travel awards for Vietnamese
Washington Monthly Magazine	2009	Prepare & publish a 12 page Special Report, "The Agent Orange Boomerang: A dark legacy of the Vietnam War is creating a whole net set of problems"
Asian American Journalists Association	2009	Panel on opportunities for fresh reporting on Agent Orange at AAJA annual meeting
East Meets West Foundation	2009	Survey of best practices for disability services & test fund-raising strategies
Institute of International Education	2009	Travel awards for Vietnamese
Tri Viet University Project	2009	Logistical support for U.S.-Vietnam Dialogue Group on Agent Orange/Dioxin
Communications Consortium Media Center	2009	Plan & convene the Agent Orange in Vietnam Information Initiative (AOVII) and conduct focus groups & national poll on Agent Orange knowledge & which messages are effective

Grant	Year	Description
War Legacies Project- AOVII	2009	Create & sustain a website with accurate & comprehensive information about Agent Orange: www.AgentOrangeRecord.org
Asian Americans & Pacific Islanders in Philanthropy- AOVII	2009	Bring Vietnamese American students & young professionals to Vietnam to learn about the Agent Orange legacy and to volunteer with NGOs providing services to disabled Vietnamese
Renaissance Journalism Center/ Zero Divide, Vietnam Reporting Project-AOVII	2009	Select, train & support 15 mainstream, Vietnamese American & student journalists to produce original news coverage of Agent Orange in Vietnam (AOVII)
Active Voice- AOVII	2009	Compare findings of the national poll on Agent Orange & existing media treatments of it & develop new messages and a social media strategy
Communications Consortium Media Center- AOVII	2010	Implement communications strategies & outreach to Congress and the media
Asian Americans & Pacific Islanders in Philanthropy- AOVII	2010	Bring Vietnamese American students & young professionals to Vietnam to learn about the Agent Orange legacy and to volunteer with NGOs providing services to disabled Vietnamese
Active Voice- AOVII	2010	Create the website www.MakeAgentOrangeHistory.org website & organize events to build public support for U.S. action on Agent Orange
Aspen Institute- AOVII	2010	Broaden & deepen public support for the Dialogue Group 2010 'Declaration & Plan of Action' on Agent Orange & monitor media impacts
Vietnam Veterans of America Foundation (VVAF)	2010	Logistical support for the US-Vietnam Dialogue Group on Agent Orange/Dioxin
East Meets West Foundation/ Thrive	2010	Create a fundraising campaign in Vietnam and internationally to further the goals of the U.S.-Vietnam Dialogue Group's Ten Year Plan
East Meets West Foundation/ Thrive	2010	Launch new website on Agent Orange directed to the Vietnamese diaspora worldwide
Vietnam Veterans of America	2010	Media outreach to link VVA work in the U.S. with the need for healthcare assistance to Vietnam

Grant	Year	Description
Institute of International Education	2010	Photographic exhibitions by Petronella Ytsma at St. Catherine University, St. Paul, Minnesota & Edgewood College, Madison, Wisconsin
Institute of International Education	2010	Logistical support for U.S.-Vietnam Dialogue Group U.S. Tour April 2010
Institute of International Education	2010	Institute of International Education- Logistical support for Common Cause Interfaith Delegation visit to Vietnam, May 2010
Common Cause Education Fund	2010	Outreach to US faith communities on Agent Orange following the Interfaith Delegation visit
Institute of International Education	2010	Logistical support for U.S.-Vietnam Dialogue Group U.S. Tour November 2010
Aspen Institute	2010	Support for Agent Orange in Vietnam Program secretariat & U.S.-Vietnam Dialogue Group
Center for Educational Exchange with Vietnam	2010	Logistical support for the U.S.- Vietnam Dialogue Group
Communications Consortium Media Center-AOVII	2011	Policy development & press and Congressional relations
Active Voice-AOVII	2011	Website enrichment and speaking events & dialogues with civic groups across the U.S.
Renaissance Journalism Center/ Zero Divide, Vietnam Reporting Project-AOVII	2011	Website dissemination of original news coverage of Agent Orange in Vietnam produced by journalists under the Vietnam Reporting Project
War Legacies Project- AOVII	2011	Advice & assistance to partners in the Agent Orange in Vietnam Information Initiative
San Francisco Rotary Club	2011	Mobilize Rotary clubs for assistance to Vietnam & Agent Orange conference at U.C.-Berkeley
East Meets West Foundation	2011	Test strategies to increase donations from individual donors for disability services in Vietnam

Fifty-Five Years of Agent Orange: Timeline of Key Statements, Decisions and Events 1961–2016

1961

U.S. President John F. Kennedy sends 3,000 military advisers, support personnel and equipment to Vietnam to support the Saigon government.

August 10, 1961

The United States tests the aerial spraying of herbicides in Kontum Province, Vietnam. Vietnam now marks August 10 every year as Agent Orange Day.

November 20, 1961

President Kennedy agrees with his advisers that the U.S. should "participate in a selective and carefully controlled joint program of defoliant operations in Vietnam starting with the clearance of key routes and proceed thereafter to food denial only if the most careful basis of resettlement and alternative food supply has been created."

January 13, 1962

First official Operation Ranch Hand spraying mission takes place along Highway 15 using C-123 aircraft.

September 22, 1962

Rachel Carson publishes *Silent Spring*, which launches the modern environmental movement in the United States.

1965

The United States sends combat forces into Vietnam.

1967

Peak year for spraying of Agent Orange in Vietnam.

April 22, 1970

First Earth Day in the United States.

May 1970

U.S. President Richard Nixon orders the end of Agent Orange spraying in Vietnam.

December 2, 1970

President Nixon signs measure establishing the U.S. Environmental Protection Agency.

January 7, 1971

The U.S. Air Force makes its last spraying mission. In September, Operation Pacer Ivy gathers remaining supplies of Agent Orange in U.S. hands. They are shipped from Vietnam to Johnston Island in the Pacific, where in 1977 they are destroyed along with remaining stocks of Agent Orange from the United States. South Vietnamese forces continue to spray the remaining stocks of Agent Blue and White until 1972.

January 28, 1973

All warring parties in the Vietnam War sign a cease-fire in Paris.
The U.S. National Academy of Sciences publishes a report finding that that use of chemical herbicides during the war has caused long-term damage to the ecology of Vietnam.

April 30, 1975

North Vietnamese forces capture Saigon and reunify Vietnam.

January 13–20, 1983

The First International Conference on herbicides used during the war takes place in Ho Chi Minh City with the participation of 160 scientists from twenty-one countries and representatives of the Food and Agricultural Organization of the United Nations, the United Nations Environment Program and UNESCO. They present seventy-two scientific papers on Agent Orange in Vietnam.

May 7, 1984

American Vietnam veterans and the U.S. chemical companies that produced Agent Orange agree to a pretrial settlement of $180 million in the veterans' lawsuit against the companies before Judge Jack Weinstein of the U.S. District Court for the Eastern District of New York.

1989

The United States creates the Leahy War Victims Fund to provide financial and technical support for Vietnamese who suffer mobility-related injuries and disabilities from anti-personnel landmines and unexploded ordnance (UXO).

October 1990

An American veteran of the Vietnam War, George Mizo; Georges Doussin of the Association Républicaine des Anciens Combattants et Victimes de Guerre; Len Aldis of the Vietnam Friendship Association in Britain and Takeo Yamanchi of the Japanese Peace Association, decide to build the Vietnam Friendship Village. The Village opens in March 1998 with six veterans and nine children as its first residents.

February 6, 1991

Congress passes the Agent Orange Act to assist American veterans of the Vietnam War who later became ill with ailments associated with presumptive exposure to dioxin.

March 1993

Susan V. Berresford, then Ford Foundation Program vice president, visits Vietnam to explore possibilities for a program to be anchored in a new Ford Foundation office in Hanoi. Among the range of topics, Vietnamese note the unresolved issue of Agent Orange.

November 15–18, 1993

The Second International Conference on herbicides used during the war takes place in Hanoi with the participation of 180 delegates from ten countries, including Australia, Britain, Germany, Japan, India, Korea, Russia and the United States.

October 1997

Susan Berresford, now president of the Ford Foundation, appoints Charles Bailey as the foundation's representative in Vietnam. Within a few months of his arrival, Bailey visits farmers in Dak Lak Province in areas sprayed with Agent Orange in the 1960s.

June 9, 1998

The Vietnam Red Cross establishes the Fund for Victims of Agent Orange in the Vietnam War to mobilize humanitarian assistance in the country to help people with health effects of Agent Orange.

October 5–9, 1998

Lieutenant General Tran Hanh, deputy minister of defense of Vietnam, meets and discusses Agent Orange with U.S. Secretary of Defense William Cohen in Washington.

March 1, 1999

Vietnam establishes the National Steering Committee for the Overcoming of Consequences of Toxic Chemicals Used by U.S. in the War in Vietnam (Committee 33). The committee comprises representatives from thirteen ministries and agencies and is tasked to "uniformly direct implementation and coordination of activities related to overcoming the consequences of toxic chemicals used by the U.S. in the war in Vietnam" (Prime Minister's Decision No. 33/1999/QD-TTg).

September 9–10, 1999

Prime Minister Phan Van Khai raises the issue of Agent Orange with U.S. President Bill Clinton at the APEC Summit Meeting in Auckland, New Zealand.

March 7, 2000

Foreign Minister Nguyen Dy Nien raises the issue of Agent Orange with U.S. Ambassador to Vietnam Pete Peterson.

March 15, 2000

President Tran Duc Luong and Prime Minister Phan Van Khai mention the issue of Agent Orange in Vietnam with visiting U.S. Secretary of Defense William Cohen.

April 2000

Hatfield Consultants, a Canadian environmental firm, and the 10-80 Committee, a research unit of the Vietnamese Ministry of Health focused on Agent Orange, complete their five-year study of dioxin levels in the soil and water throughout the Aluoi Valley, Thua Thien-Hue Province. They report high levels of TCDD dioxin in soil, fish fat and duck fat, and in blood and breast milk samples taken from people living on a former U.S. military base in the valley. This study became the basis for the dioxin hot spots hypothesis, that dioxin remains at dangerous levels largely at former U.S. bases.

May 23, 2000

Vietnam issues policies for assisting participants in the war who were exposed to chemicals and were no longer capable of work and for their children born with deformities (Prime Minister's Decision No. 26/2000/QD-TTg).

May 27, 2000

Vietnam's Ministry of Labor, Invalids and Social Affairs (MOLISA) surveys people suffering the consequences of exposure to wartime chemicals in 45 districts of 16 provinces. The findings paint the current situation of Agent Orange victims in Vietnam: multiple diseases and ailments, limited capacity for education and work, a difficult life and under-resourced treatment and care.

June 2000

Ford Foundation Trustees and president Berresford visit Vietnam. In a meeting with Deputy Prime Minister Nguyen Manh Cam they endorse Charles Bailey's recommendation of a grant of $150,000 to the Red Cross Agent Orange Victims Fund. This action launches Ford Foundation efforts to find a solution to the Agent Orange/dioxin issue.

November 17–18, 2000

President Bill Clinton visits Hanoi and meets with General Secretary Le Kha Phieu; President Tran Duc Luong; Prime Minister Pham Van Khai; the chairman of the Vietnamese Red Cross; Nguyen Trong Nhan and students at Hanoi National University. The Vietnamese raise the Agent Orange issue, and Clinton acknowledges a continued responsibility to heal the wounds of war.

November 27–December 1, 2000

U.S. and Vietnamese officials and scientists meet in Singapore to discuss joint research on the impact of dioxin on human health and environment. The two sides disagree on approach and methods to resolving this issue and the meeting ends without result.

January 9, 2001

Professor Hoang Dinh Cau, former chairman of the 10-80 Committee, requests that Prime Minister Phan Van Khai end previous secrecy and openly publish the findings of seven years of Vietnam-Japan research on Agent Orange. In June the Minister of Science, Technology and Environment establishes an editorial board for a white paper on Agent Orange. The board comprises forty-one scientists and state managers in medicine, biology, chemistry and environment. Professor Hoang Dinh Cau is chairman and editor, but the white paper is not produced, and he dies in 2005.

July 2–6, 2001

Dr. Nguyen Ngoc Sinh, the first director of the Office of Committee 33, leads a delegation of scientists to the United States to work with Dr. Christopher Portier, director of the National Toxicology Program, and deputy director, National Institute of Environment Health Sciences, and a team of American scientists. The two sides agree on a Vietnam-U.S. scientific conference and a pilot study on biological remediation of soils and sediments contaminated with dioxin.

March 2002

Scientists from Vietnam, the United States and eleven other countries meet at the Daewoo Hotel in Hanoi to discuss the latest research on the effects of dioxin on human health and the environment. A consultative workshop following the conference prioritized studies of the impact of dioxin on exposed populations, therapies to reduce dioxin levels in humans and the concentrations and fate of dioxins at former American bases. The two governments agree on a mechanism for planning and funding joint research and for exchange of scientists. The agreement, however, lacks specific commitments and assignment of specific responsibilities, and the outcomes are therefore meager.

June 7, 2002

Dr. Kenneth Olden, director of the U.S. National Institute of Environmental Health Sciences, writes to Pham Khoi Nguyen, vice minister of science, technology and environment and deputy chairman of Committee 33, to propose joint research on the impact of dioxin on human health and the environment.

July 28, 2002

Over sixty experts in the natural and social sciences, public health and related fields meet in Stockholm for the Environmental Conference on Cambodia, Laos and Vietnam. The Conference Declaration calls for a large-scale effort to address the present and continuing impact of war on the lives, livelihoods and environment of the peoples of Indochina.

September 2002

A Ford Foundation grant provides $289,000 to the 10-80 Committee, Ministry of Health. The committee uses the funds to collaborate with Hatfield Consultants in the first assessment of possible dioxin residues at all 2,735 former U.S. military installations throughout central and southern Vietnam.

June 6, 2003

U.S. Deputy Secretary of State Richard Armitage meets Deputy Foreign Minister Nguyen Dinh Bin in Washington, acknowledges Vietnam's request for assistance with dioxin and proposes the two countries move forward with the proposals put forth at the March 2002 Daewoo conference.

July 3, 2003

Following the Armitage meeting, Deputy Foreign Minister Nguyen Dinh Bin meets with Ambassador Raymond F. Burghardt to discuss cooperation on research and technical projects and the early formation of a Joint Advisory Committee between the two countries.

October 2003

The Institute of International Relations in Hanoi and the Johns Hopkins School of Advanced International Studies in Washington put Agent Orange on the agenda at a bilateral conference on "The Future of the U.S.-Vietnam Relationship" at the Carnegie Endowment for Peace in Washington. The participants include officials of both countries and others from academia, the Vietnamese American community, nongovernmental organizations and the American business community. The academic setting and inclusion of unofficial participants permit easier discussion of Agent Orange.

January 30, 2004

The Vietnam Association of Victims of Agent Orange and twenty-seven individual Vietnamese file suit in U.S. Federal Court for the Eastern District of New York against the American companies that manufactured Agent Orange and similar herbicides for the U.S. government during the Vietnam War.

April 30, 2004

Lewis M. Stern, director for Southeast Asia in the U.S. Department of Defense, writes to Senior Colonel Nguyen Ngoc Giao, military attaché of Vietnam in the United States. Stern reminds Giao that in 1995 the United States and Vietnam settled all government and private claims related to the war, and therefore the United States would not be responsible for damages alleged to have been related to Agent Orange. He adds that American law barred the Department of Defense from participating in the dioxin cleanup. However, the Defense Department can give Vietnam the records of the spraying program, provide information on remediation technologies and share the department's experience with managing dioxin contamination in the United States.

June 2004

The State University of New York at Albany and the Hanoi Medical University plan to carry out a $3-million study of the epidemiology of birth defects in Vietnam, funded by the National Institute of Environmental Health Sciences. In the event, the Americans and Vietnamese are unable to agree on its design and conduct, and the institute cancels the grant in March 2005.

March 11, 2005

An international conference is held in Paris on the consequences of Agent Orange in Vietnam.

June 2005

Vietnam's Defense Minister Pham Van Tra meets U.S. Secretary of Defense Donald Rumsfeld in Washington and asks him to provide information on Agent Orange and Operation Ranch Hand to the Vietnamese. Rumsfeld agrees and the Department of Defense and Ministry of Defense hold a workshop August 16-18, 2005, to exchange technical information, archival data and experience with dioxin remediation in the United States.

November 2005

Professor Dang Vu Minh, chair, Vietnam Institute of Science and Technology; Dr. William Farland, deputy administrator for research, U.S. Environmental Protection Agency, and U.S. Ambassador Michael W. Marine inaugurate a laboratory for dioxin analysis at the Vietnam Academy of Science and Technology. Key equipment for the lab is donated by the U.S. Centers for Disease Control.

January 9, 2006

Ambassador Michael W. Marine writes to Pham Khoi Nguyen, deputy chairman of Committee 33, to introduce an EPA scientist, Vance S. Fong, to work with the Ministry of Defense, the Office of Committee 33 and the BEM Systems on plans for remediation at the Da Nang Airport.

February 2006

The 10-80 Committee and Hatfield present the results of their survey to locate and quantify the toxicity of dioxin hot spots at former U.S. military bases. These findings strengthen Vietnamese determination to address the issue head-on with the U.S. government.

June 5–6, 2006

The Joint Advisory Committee (JAC), a forum for the exchange of technical and scientific information on dioxin remediation and health and disability, holds its first meeting. The JAC will meet in Vietnam every year for eight years from 2006 through 2014. On the American side the first JAC members are Dr. William Farland (EPA, co-chair), Dr. Anne P. Sassaman (National Institute of Environmental Health Sciences), Colonel Mark Chakwin (military attaché, U.S. Embassy), Dr. Marie Sweeney (health attaché, U.S. Embassy), and Nathan Sage (environment officer, U.S. Embassy).

The Vietnamese members are Dr. Le Ke Son (Committee 33, cochair), Professor Tran Van Sung (Institute of Chemistry, Vietnam Academy of Science and Technology), Dr. Pham Quoc Bao (Department of Science and Training, Ministry of Health), Pham Van Que (Americas Department, Ministry of Foreign Affairs), and Major General Nguyen Ngoc Duong (Department of Science, Technology and Environment, Ministry of Defense).

July 2006

The Ford Foundation begins a multiyear program of grants for projects to assist Vietnamese with disabilities, remediate dioxin-contaminated soils and educate Americans about the continuing challenge of Agent Orange in Vietnam. By the time the program concludes in 2011, the foundation will have provided $17 million in grants for these purposes.

August 2006

Vietnamese scientists present their research on Agent Orange/dioxin in papers accepted by the 26th International Symposium on Halogenated Persistent Organic Pollutants in Oslo, Norway.

November 12, 2006

On the eve of U.S. President George W. Bush's visit to Vietnam, the *Washington Post* publishes a front-page story on Agent Orange. (Anthony Faiola, "In Vietnam, Old Foes Take Aim at War's Toxic Legacy," *Washington Post*, November 12, 2006). The Ford Foundation holds a press conference in Hanoi to announce major new grant making in this area.

November 17, 2006

At the conclusion of President Bush's visit, he and President Nguyen Minh Triet issue a joint statement that for the first time officially acknowledges the dioxin issue, saying "President Triet also expressed appreciation for the U.S. government's increasing development assistance to Vietnam and urged the U.S. side to increase humanitarian assistance including through co-operation on areas such as unexploded ordnance and continued assistance to Vietnamese with disabilities. The United States and Vietnam also agreed that further joint efforts to address the environmental contamination near former dioxin storage sites would make a valuable contribution to the continued development of their bilateral relationship."

December 19–22, 2006

Tim Rieser, the key Democratic majority staff member of the Senate Appropriations Committee, Subcommittee on State, Foreign Operations and Related Programs; and Bobby Muller, president, Vietnam Veterans of America Foundation, visit Vietnam and meet with U.S. Ambassador Michael W. Marine; the deputy chief of mission, Jonathan Aloisi; Dr. Le Ke Son, Committee 33; Charles R. Bailey, Ford Foundation, and others. At a Hanoi press conference Rieser announces that the United States has a "shared responsibility" to address unresolved issues from the war.

April 2007

Dr. Le Ke Son leads Vietnamese delegation to Washington and New York to meet officials and discuss how an initial Congressional appropriation will be used.

February 5–9, 2007

A citizens' committee of prominent Vietnamese and Americans, called the U.S.-Vietnam Dialogue Group on Agent Orange/Dioxin, forms and meets in Vietnam with the Ford Foundation president, Susan V. Berresford, as its convener. The founder co-chairs are Walter Isaacson, president of the Aspen Institute, and Ton Nu Thi Ninh, vice chair of the Foreign Affairs Committee of Vietnam's National Assembly. The Dialogue Group calls for a humanitarian response to Agent Orange, aims to mainstream the Agent Orange issue in the United States, and seeks to mobilize new resources for five priority tasks. Over the next seven years, the Dialogue Group alternates sessions in Vietnam and the United States, meets with affected families, reviews projects, publishes reports and holds press conferences. In June 2010 the Dialogue Group releases its Declaration and Plan of Action, calling for a joint effort of the two countries over the next ten years at a cost of $350 million.

February 2007

U.S. Ambassador Michael W. Marine secures a State Department grant and counterpart funds from the Environmental Protection Agency of $400,000 toward the cost of dioxin remediation at Da Nang.

July 24, 2007

U.S. Ambassador Michael W. Marine, his wife, Carmella, and Ken Fairfax, U.S. consul-general, visit the dioxin-contaminated area at the Da Nang Airport with Dr. Le Ke Son, director, Office of Committee 33, and Colonel Tran Ngoc Tam, head of environment, science and technology, Ministry of Defense.

August 24, 2007

United Nations Development Program/Vietnam allocates $350,000 for a project for "capacity building and preparation of a master plan for the rehabilitation of the environment in dioxin hot spots in Vietnam."

February 2008

The State Department designates USAID to administer funds appropriated by the Congress for Agent Orange in Vietnam.

February 20, 2008

Vietnam's minister of health issues a list of diseases and disabilities related to exposure to Agent Orange/dioxin (Decision No. 09/2008/QD-BYT).

February 2008

The president of the U.S. Fund for UNICEF, Caryl Stern, and the fund's board members visit Vietnam. By June the fund has raised $2.3 million for a new UNICEF program for children with disabilities in Vietnam.

May 15, 2008

Eni Faleomavaega, chair of the U.S. House of Representatives Subcommittee on Asia Pacific and Global Environment, holds a hearing on "Our Forgotten Responsibility: What Can We Do to Help Victims of Agent Orange?" Four members of the U.S. Vietnam Dialogue Group on Agent Orange/Dioxin testify and the 10-80 Committee/Hatfield survey of dioxin hot spots is placed in the *Congressional Record*.

May 2008

Office of Committee 33 hosts a scientific conference with EPA, UNDP, U.S. Embassy and BEM to review the pilot effort to remediate dioxin on the Bien Hoa Air Base and to examine alternative technologies.

June 25, 2008

Prime Minister Nguyen Tan Dung meets President George W. Bush in Washington. Their joint statement says: "The prime minister welcomes bilateral efforts in dealing with environmental pollution in areas near former U.S. military bases and especially the disbursement of $3 million by the United States to provide health projects and environmental restoration."

October 29, 2008

USAID announces commitment of the first $1 million of the $3 million appropriated by Congress in 2007 for cleanup of dioxin hot spots and health programs in surrounding communities. The funds go to three American NGOs (East Meets West Foundation, Save the Children and Vietnam Assistance for the Handicapped) for a range of direct services to children with disabilities in selected districts in Da Nang City.

February 24–25, 2009

Office of Committee 33 and UNDP host the first workshop drawing together the principal stakeholders in the cleanup of environmental dioxin: Committee 33, Ministry of Defense, U.S. State Department, EPA and Czech Republic. Participants share data on the principal dioxin hot spots in Vietnam funded by various sources — Da Nang (Ford Foundation), Phu Cat and Bien Hoa (UNDP) — and reach conclusions about cleanup strategies for all three locations.

March 2009

President Obama signs an appropriations bill that contains $3 million "for assistance for Vietnam to continue environmental remediation and related health programs at dioxin-contaminated sites."

March 2009

The U.S. Supreme Court declines to hear an appeal of the Vietnamese lawsuit against the companies that manufactured Agent Orange and similar herbicides.

May 2009

Technical experts of American EPA and the Vietnam Academy of Science and Technology launch a pilot project to test bioremediation of dioxin at the Da Nang Airport.

May 18, 2009

The Vietnam Ministry of Natural Resources and Environment establishes the Dioxin Laboratory in the ministry at a cost of $6.75 million. Atlantic Philanthropies and the Bill and Melinda Gates Foundation provide $5.3 million in grant support for the project; the government of Vietnam funds the balance.

June 4, 2009

Eni Faleomavaega, chair of the U.S. House of Representatives Subcommittee on Asia Pacific and Global Environment, holds a second hearing on Agent Orange/Dioxin in Vietnam. Scot Marciel, deputy assistant secretary of state for East Asia & Pacific, testifies, as do members of the U.S.-Vietnam Dialogue Group.

June 17, 2010

Vietnam's National Assembly approves the Law on Disability, which establishes the rights of people with disabilities, including Agent Orange victims (No. 51/2010 / QH 12).

June 28, 2010

Vietnam's Natural Resources Minister, Pham Khoi Nguyen, and the UNDP resident coordinator, John Hendra, sign an agreement for a $4,977,000 global environmental facility project to remediate 7,500 cubic meters of dioxin-contaminated soils into a passive landfill in a remote area of the Phu Cat Airport. Funds are also allocated to assess the status of dioxin at the Bien Hoa Air Base, isolate it to prevent its further spread, compare alternative cleanup technologies, compile and publish previous research on dioxin and hold scientific conferences.

July 6, 2010

U.S. Senators Tom Harkin and Bernie Sanders visit the Da Nang Airport and a rehabilitation hospital with Charles Bailey. This is the first time for voting members of Congress to investigate the environmental and human consequences of Agent Orange on the ground.

July 22, 2010

At a press conference in Hanoi, Secretary of State Hillary Clinton says, "The minister and I discussed the concern that both Vietnam and the United States have about Agent Orange and the consequences that it produced in the people here. . . . I told the minister that I would work to increase our cooperation and make even greater progress together."

September 2010

Senator Patrick Leahy places a statement on Agent Orange in the *Congressional Record*, writing that "it would be hard to overstate the importance the Vietnamese give to addressing the needs of people who have been harmed."

September 2010

Thuy Vu, a newscaster at KPIX Channel 5 in San Francisco, reports on Agent Orange from Vietnam for CBS News http://www.youtube.com/watch?v=kkbnFfldsOc. Her report receives numerous journalism awards.

September 28, 2010

Ambassador Michael W. Michalak writes to Nguyen Huy Hieu, Deputy Minister of Defense, with the Draft Project Plan to remediate dioxin in Da Nang from 2011 to 2013.

October 2010

Secretary Hillary Clinton returns to Hanoi and announces U.S. support to completely clean up the dioxin-contaminated soil at the Da Nang airport, the first of the three principal dioxin hot spots.

January 30, 2011

Pulitzer Prize winners Connie Schultz and Nick Ut publish an eight-page special report on Agent Orange in the *Cleveland Plain Dealer* (http://bit.ly/fP59JT).

March 2011

Bob Edgar, the president of Common Cause, an American advocacy NGO, leads a delegation to Vietnam. The delegation includes Americans prominent in the fields of public policy, public health, the environment and disabilities movements, and religion.

April 14, 2011

Congress appropriates $18.5 million in new funding to continue Agent Orange activities in Vietnam. Of this amount, $15.5 million will underwrite the decontamination of the Da Nang dioxin hot spot; $3 million is reserved for related health activities.

August 2011

The Aspen Institute, Da Nang City government, Cam Le District government, Children of Vietnam and the Rockefeller Foundation create the Public Private Partnership (PPP) in Da Nang. The PPP continues a district-level rolling reform of social services for children and young adults with disabilities and is the first application of the PPP model to funding disabilities programs in Vietnam.

August 29, 2011

The Minister of Science and Technology approves the objectives, contents and expected outcomes of the research program to overcome the consequences of Agent Orange/dioxin (Decision No. 2631/ QD-BKHCN).

October 19, 2011

Vietnam's minister of science and technology appoints Dr. Le Ke Son to chair the management board overseeing thirteen new state research projects on Agent Orange/dioxin (Decision No. 3242/QD).

October 28–29, 2011

One hundred sixty students at the University of California/Berkeley, Vietnamese Americans, members of the U.S.-Vietnam Dialogue Group and members of Rotary participate in the Rotary Peace Conference on Agent Orange and Addressing the Legacy of the War in Vietnam.

December 22, 2011

President Obama signs the 2012 Consolidated Appropriations Act, which allocates $20 million for Agent Orange in Vietnam. Of this total, $15 million is intended to complete the funding of the full remediation of the Da Nang Airport dioxin hot spot and to get a start on remediating Bien Hoa and possibly other hot spots. The balance of $5 million is for health/disabilities programs in areas of Vietnam that were targeted with Agent Orange or remain contaminated with dioxin.

December 30, 2011

USAID releases a Request for Assistance seeking bids for a three-year program of services to people with disabilities at $3 million a year for a total of $9 million. Seventy percent of the funds are to be used for programs in Da Nang; 40 percent of the funds are to go for direct services to people with disabilities.

June 1, 2012

Vietnam's prime minister approves the "National Action Plan to overcome the basic consequences of toxic chemicals used by the U.S. in the war in Vietnam to 2015 and vision 2020" to guide ministries in addressing the Agent Orange legacy (Decision No. 651/QD-TTg).

June 27, 2012

Frank Donovan, director of USAID Vietnam, writes to Nguyen Xuan Tien, deputy director of foreign economic relations in the Ministry of Planning and Investment, that USAID will conduct an environmental assessment of dioxin contamination at the Bien Hoa Airport.

July 2012

The Dialogue Group and Rotary International inaugurate a piped water system that they funded in Dong Son Commune, Aluoi District, Thua Thien-Hue Province. The system brings filtered water to all 259 households in the commune, which lies near a former U.S. military base where Agent Orange was used during the war.

July 16, 2012

The National Assembly amends several articles of the ordinance on assistance to those who have contributed to the revolution, specifically to victims of toxic chemicals (Ordinance No. 26/2005/PL-UBTVQH 11 & Ordinance No. 35/2007/PL-11).

August 9, 2012

The governments of the United States and Vietnam break ground on what is expected to be a four-year, $43-million project to clean 73,000 cubic meters of dioxin-contaminated soils at the Da Nang Airport. The ground-breaking is a matter of great satisfaction and celebration for Americans and Vietnamese, and a milestone in the relations between Vietnam and the United States.

October 2012

USAID launches a three-year, $9-million disability-support project for Da Nang, Bien Hoa and Phu Cat.

January 2013

The cost to clean up the dioxin at the Da Nang airport becomes clearer as work proceeds; the estimate increases to $84 million from $43 million.

March 2013

A staff delegation from the U.S. Congress visits the Bien Hoa Air Base, meets with a Dialogue Group member, Dr. Nguyen Thi Ngoc Phuong, at the Peace Village in Ho Chi Minh City, confers with the Vietnam Association of Victims of Agent Orange and visits other impacted areas in central Vietnam.

April 26, 2013

Vietnam's prime minister approves a project to take care of orphans and helpless, abandoned children, children with HIV/AIDS, children who are victims of toxic chemicals, children with severe disabilities and children affected by disaster for period 2013–2020 (Decision No. 647/QD-TTg).

May 2013

UNICEF dedicates its 2013 Report on the State of the World's Children to children with disabilities. UNICEF's executive director, Anthony Lake, and Vietnamese Vice President Nguyen Thi Doan launch the report in Da Nang.

July 15, 2013

The dialogue group convener, Susan V. Berresford, writes to U.S. Secretary of State John F. Kerry on the eve of President Truong Tan Sang's visit to Washington. She urges the secretary to press forward on addressing the full range of disability issues in Vietnam that stem from conflicts, poverty and limited health care services. Secretary Kerry replies, "I assure you that the United States is committed to helping Vietnam build a sustainable system of comprehensive, integrated services for Vietnamese with disabilities, regardless of cause."

July 25, 2013

President Barack Obama and President Truong Tan Sang meet at the White House and agree to open a new phase of bilateral relations by forming a U.S.-Vietnam Comprehensive Partnership as a framework for advancing the relationship. In the joint statement following the meeting, President Obama reaffirms "the United States' commitment to providing further medical and other care and assistance for persons with disabilities, regardless of cause."

November 13, 2014

Prime Minister Nguyen Tan Dung and President Barack Obama meet at the ASEAN 25th Summit in Myanmar. Obama confirms that the United States will continue to assist Vietnam with the remediation of dioxin.

December 12, 2014

Senator Patrick Leahy writes to President Truong Tan Sang about American assistance for remediation of the Da Nang Airport and for Vietnamese with disabilities and also notes a continuing concern about human rights in Vietnam.

June 23, 2015

Senator Patrick Leahy gives a speech on "Addressing Agent Orange in Vietnam" at the Center for Strategic and International Studies, Washington, D.C., followed by a panel discussion with Tim Rieser, Le Ke Son, Michael Martin and Charles Bailey.

December 18, 2015

The U.S. Congress passes the Consolidated Appropriations Act of 2016, which stipulates that "Funds . . . shall be made available for remediation of dioxin-contaminated sites in Vietnam and may be made available to the government of Vietnam, including the military, for such purposes. Funds . . . shall be made available for health and disability programs in areas sprayed with Agent Orange and otherwise contaminated with dioxin, to assist individuals with severe upper or lower body mobility impairment and/or cognitive or developmental disabilities."

February 29, 2016

Courtney Marsh's film *Chau, Beyond the Lines* is a finalist for an Academy Award in the short documentary category. The film depicts the successful struggle of Le Minh Chau, born with deformities linked to Agent Orange, to become an artist. American Ambassador Ted Osius screens the film at American centers in Hanoi and Ho Chi Minh City.

May 24, 2016

President Barack Obama visits Vietnam and in a speech in Hanoi declares, "Even as we continue to assist Vietnamese with disabilities, including children, we are also continuing to help remove Agent Orange-dioxin."

May 31, 2017

President Donald J. Trump and Prime Minister Nguyen Xuan Phuc meet and discuss measures to expand joint work in humanitarian cooperation and war legacies.

NOTES

Introduction: The Aftermath of War

1. The literature on the Vietnam War is voluminous. Two good starting points are Christopher Goscha, *Vietnam: A New History*, Basic Books, New York, 2016; and Leslie H. Gelb and Richard K. Betts, *The Irony of Vietnam: The System Worked*, Brookings, Washington, D.C., 2016.

2. National Academies of Sciences, Engineering, and Medicine. *Veterans and Agent Orange: Update 2014*. Washington, D.C.: The National Academies Press, 2016. http://www.nationalacademies.org/hmd/Reports/2016/Veterans-and-Agent-Orange-Update-2014.aspx. Key Vietnamese studies are described later in this book.

3. 26th International Symposium on Halogenated Persistent Organic Pollutants, Oslo, Norway, 2006. The Symposium is the annual apex peer review meeting of scientists worldwide who work on persistent organic pollutants (POPs). Vietnamese scientists have presented their current research at the symposium every year since 2006.

4. Dioxin Laboratory, Center for Environmental Monitoring, Vietnam Environmental Administration, Hanoi, 2009.

5. Michael F. Martin, "Vietnamese Victims of Agent Orange and U.S.-Vietnam Relations," Congressional Research Service, August 29, 2012, https://fas.org/sgp/crs/row/RL34761.pdf.

Essay: How We Got Here and What's Next

1. Joint Statement of Presidents George W. Bush and Nguyen Minh Triet, Hanoi, November 17, 2006.

2. H.R. 933 — Consolidated and Further Continuing Appropriations Act, 2013.

3. H.R. 2029 — Consolidated Appropriations Act, 2016.

4. U.S. Department of State, "U.S. Relations With Vietnam," Bureau of East Asian and Pacific Affairs Fact Sheet, August 25, 2016. Emphasis added.

5. Clay Risen, "The Environmental Consequences of War: Why militaries almost never clean up the messes they leave behind," *Washington Monthly*, January/February 2010, A8.

6. Risen, "Environmental Consequences."

7. Interview with Walter Isaacson, president and CEO, Aspen Institute and American co-chair, U.S.-Vietnam Dialogue Group on Agent Orange/ Dioxin, Washington, D.C., April 30, 2015.

8. Interview with Ambassador Ton Nu Thi Ninh, former deputy chair, Foreign Affairs Committee, National Assembly of Vietnam and Vietnamese co-chair, U.S.-Vietnam Dialogue Group on Agent Orange/ Dioxin, Ho Chi Minh City, Vietnam, January 12, 2016.

9. Christopher B. Whitney, "Soft Power in Asia: Results of a 2008 Multinational Survey of Public Opinion," The Chicago Council on Global Affairs, 2009, 12.

10. Prashanth Parameswaran, "Third U.S. warship visits Vietnam's Cam Ranh International Port: Visit a reminder of the increased defense collaboration between the two sides," Diplomat, December 16, 2016, http://thediplomat.com/2016/12/ third-us-warship-visits-vietnams-cam-ranh-international-port/.

Chapter 1: Is There Still Dioxin Pollution in Southern Vietnam?

1. Government of Vietnam, Ministry of Natural Resources and Environment, "National Technical Regulations on Allowed Limits of Dioxin in Soils," QCVN 45:2012/BTNMT, Hanoi, 2012.

2. Ministry of Natural Resources and Environment, National Research Program KHCN-33/11-15, "Report on Research on the Impact of Agent Orange/Dioxin on Environment," Hanoi, 2012.

3. L. W. Dwernychuk, et al., "Dioxin reservoirs in southern Viet Nam — A legacy of Agent Orange," Chemosphere 47 (2002): 117–137.

4. Government of Vietnam, "National Technical Regulation on Allowed Limits."

5. U. S. Agency for International Development, "Environmental Assessment of Dioxin Contamination at Bien Hoa Air Base — Environmental Assessment — Final," CDM International Inc. and Hatfield Consultants, May 3, 2016, 46–47.

6. Office of the National Steering Committee 33, Ministry of Natural Resources and the Environment (MONRE) and Hatfield Consultants, "Environmental and Human Health Assessment of Dioxin Contamination at Bien Hoa Air Base, Vietnam," Final Report, August 2011, 1–19.

7. Arthur H. Westing, "Ecocidal Warfare (& Related) Publications (1967–2008)," Westing Associates in Environment, Security & Education, Putney, Vermont, http://www.agentorangerecord.com/images/uploads/ modules/Ecocide_refs_-_AHW.pdf.

8. Arnold Schecter, et al. "Agent Orange and the Vietnamese: The Persistence of Elevated Dioxin Levels in Human Tissues," *American Journal of Public Health* 85, no. 4 (April 1995): 516–522, http://www.agentorangerecord.com/images/uploads/resources/studies/AJPH(2)%201995.pdf.

9. J. M. Stellman, et al. "The extent and patterns of usage of Agent Orange and other herbicides in Vietnam," *Nature* 422 (April 2003): 681–687, and personal communication.

10. Stellman, "extent and patterns," and personal communication.

11. Stellman, "extent and patterns."

12. Ibid.

13. Findings for Quang Tri, Thua Thien-Hue, Kon Tum, Binh Duong, Binh Phuoc, Tay Ninh, Dong Nai, Ho Chi Minh City, Cau Mau, Nha Trang and Saigon River are in Ministry of Natural Resources and Environment, National Research Program KHCN-33/11-15, "Report of Research on Impact of Agent Orange/Dioxin on the Environment," Hanoi, 2012.

14. Every year Vietnam marks August 10 as Agent Orange Day, commemorating the day in 1961 when the United States began its program of spraying herbicides in Vietnam.

15. Dwernychuk, et al., *"Dioxin reservoirs."*

16. L. W. Dwernychuk, "Dioxin hotspots in Vietnam — Short Communication," *Chemosphere* 60 (2005): 998–999.

17. Hatfield Consultants Partnership and 10-80 Committee, Ministry of Health, Vietnam, "Identification of New Agent Orange/Dioxin Contamination Hot Spots in Southern Vietnam — Final Report," January 2006, x.

18. Findings for A So, Ta Bat, Tan Son Nhat, Phan Rang, Nha Trang and Tuy Hoa are reported in Ministry of Defense, "Analysis of Dioxin Contamination in Former Military Air Bases," Z-9, Hanoi, November 2010.

19. Findings for Pleiku and Vam Cong, are reported in Ministry of Defense, "Evaluation of Dioxins/Furans and Dioxin-like Pollutants in Peiku Airport, Gia Lai Province and Vam Cong Airport, An Giang Province," Hanoi, November 2013.

20. UNDP/GEF, "Results of Dioxin Analysis at Spray Plane Crash Site, Thua Thien-Hue," Project for Management of Dioxin Hotspots in Vietnam, Hanoi, January 2012.

21. Arnold Schecter, L. C. Dai, O. Päpke, J. Prange, J. D. Constable, M. Matsuda, V. D. Thao, A. L. Piskac, "Recent dioxin contamination from Agent Orange in residents of a Southern Vietnam city," *Journal of Occupational & Environmental Medicine* 43 (2001): 435–443.

22. Office of Steering Committee 33, Ministry of Natural Resources and the Environment (MONRE), "Comprehensive Report — Agent Orange/Dioxin Contamination at Three Hotspots: Bien Hoa, Da Nang and Phu Cat Air Bases," updated November 2013, 49-52.

23. Office of Steering Committee 33, MONRE, "Comprehensive Report . . . Three Hotspots," 42.

24. U. S. Agency for International Development, "Environmental Assessment."

25. Ibid., Figure 2-1, 50.

26. For a detailed description of these techniques, see ibid., 129–144.

27. "At this stage of the alternatives evaluation, the design for the project alternatives are very conceptual and there are many uncertainties. To account for this, accuracy ranges are applied [to] the estimated costs. The ranges applied to the Bien Hoa EA (-40% to +75%) are based on USEPA guidance for developing cost estimates for Superfund/remediation projects in the U.S." U. S. Agency for International Development, "Environmental Assessment," 25–27, 33.

28. U. S. Agency for International Development, "Environmental Assessment," 10.

29. Office of Steering Committee 33, MONRE, "Comprehensive Report . . . Three Hotspots," 73.

30. Office of the National Steering Committee 33, MONRE and Hatfield Consultants, "Comprehensive Assessment of Dioxin Contamination in Da Nang Airport, Viet Nam: Environmental Levels, Human Exposure and Options for Mitigating Impacts — Final Summary of Findings," November 2009.

31. T. G. Boivin, et al., "Agent Orange Dioxin Contamination in the Environment and Food Chain at Key Hot Spots in Viet Nam: Da Nang, Bien Hoa and Phu Cat," paper presented at the 31st International Symposium on Halogenated Persistent Organic Pollutants, Brussels, August 21–25, 2011.

32. Dwernychuk, et al., "Dioxin reservoirs," 117–137.

33. Boivin, et al., "Agent Orange Dioxin Contamination."

34. J. T. Durant, T. G. Boivin, H. R. Pohl, T. Sinks, "Public health assessment of dioxin contaminated fish at former U.S. air base, Bien Hoa, Viet Nam," *International Journal of Environmental Health Research* 25, no. 3 (2015): 254–264, http://dx.doi.org/10.1080/09603123.2014.938026.

35. M. H. Nguyen, et al., "Dioxin concentrations in human blood and breast milk near key hotspots in Vietnam: Da Nang and Bien Hoa," Paper presented at the 31st International Symposium on Halogenated Persistent Pollutants, Brussels, August 21–25, 2011.

36. Funding for the study came from UNDP/Global Environmental Fund under the project Dioxin Treatment in Heavily Contaminated Areas. The Atlantic Philanthropies, the Bill and Melinda Gates Foundation and the government of Vietnam jointly funded the construction and equipping of the Dioxin Laboratory for the Vietnam Environment Administration.

37. Nguyen Hung Minh, et al., "Research to identify the concentration and movement of dioxin from Agent Orange in Bien Hoa and Da Nang and distinguish dioxin from Agent Orange and other sources of emissions and propose solutions to prevent dioxin exposure," *Research on Overcoming the Consequences of Agent Orange/Dioxin Used by the U.S. in the War on Environment and Human Health in Vietnam*, National Research Program of Science and Technology, 2011–2015, Hanoi, October 2015.

38. Nguyen Hung Minh, et al., "Dioxin Emissions From Industry and Waste Treatment," report published by Office 33, UNDP/Global Environmental Fund, Program on Dioxin treatment in hotspots in Vietnam, 2014.

39. Vu Chien Thang, "Identification of Dioxin Levels from Agent Orange and Other Sources in Human Blood and Common Foods in Different Areas of Vietnam," *Research on Overcoming the Consequences of Agent Orange/Dioxin Used by the U.S. in the War on Environment and Human Health in Vietnam*, National Research Program of Science and Technology, 2011–2015, Hanoi, October 2015.

40. Nguyen Hung Minh et al., "Research for identifying the remaining and spreading of Agent Orange dioxin in Bien Hoa and Da Nang and the difference in characteristics of dioxin from other sources," under the Science and Technology Research Program KHCN-33/11-15, 2014.

Chapter 2: Who Has Been Exposed to Agent Orange/Dioxin, and How Many Victims of Agent Orange Are There in Vietnam?

1. Jeanne Mager Stellman, Steven D. Stellman, Richard Christian, Tracy Weber and Carrie Tomasallo, "Extent and patterns of usage of Agent Orange and other herbicides in Vietnam," *Nature* 422 (April 2003): 681–687.

2. Nguyen Van Tuong, "Analysis of Dioxin in Blood and Milk of People Living in Sprayed Areas in Thua Thien-Hue and Da Nang Compared With Dioxin in Blood and Milk of People Living in Hai Phong," Japanese National Institute for Environmental Health, Fukuoka, 2004.

3. Hatfield Consultants and Office of National Steering Committee 33, "Comprehensive Assessment of Dioxin Contamination in Da Nang Airport, Vietnam: Environmental Levels, Human Exposure and Options for Mitigating Impacts Final Summary of Findings," November 2009, 2, 4; Nguyen Van Tuong, "Environmental and Human Health Assessment of Dioxin Contamination at Bien Hoa Air Base, Vietnam: Final Report," August 2011, 3–43.

4. Le Bach Quang, et al. "Nghien Cuu dich te hoc benh tat cua 47,000 cuu chien binh co phoi nhiem CDC va so sanh voi nhom cuu chien binh khong phoi nhiem," CDC, Hoc Vien Quan Y, Hanoi, 2005. ("Epidemiological study of the diseases of 47,000 war veterans exposed to Agent Orange and compared with group of veterans who were not exposed to Agent Orange," Military Medical University, Hanoi, 2005).

5. J. N. Robinson, K. A. Fox, W. G. Jackson, N. S. Ketchum, M. Pavuk, and W. Grubbs, "Air Force Health Study — An Overview," *J. Organohalogen Compounds* 68 (2006): 752–755.

6. Joel E. Michalek and Ram C. Tripathi, "Pharmacokinetics of TCDD in Veterans of Operation Ranch Hand: 15 Year Follow-up," *Journal of Toxicology and Environmental Health* 57, Part A, no. 6 (1999): 369–78.

7. Hatfield Consultants and Office of National Steering Committee 33, "Assessment of Dioxin Contamination in the Environment and Human Population in the Vicinity of Da Nang Air Base, Vietnam Report 3: Final Report," April 2007.

8. Ministry of Health, Decision No.09/2008/QD-BYT, February 20, 2008.

9. U.S. Department of Veterans Affairs, Annual Benefits Report 2015, http://www.benefits.va.gov/REPORTS/abr/ABR-Compensation-FY15-05092016.pdf.

10. U.S. Department of Veterans Affairs via Charles Ornstein, ProPublica, personal communication, January 3, 2017.

11. The 10-80 Committee, or Committee for Investigating the Consequences of Toxic Chemicals Used by the U.S. in the War in Vietnam, was created in October 1980 and reported to the prime minister. When Committee 33 was created in 1999, the 10-80 Committee was moved to the Ministry of Health and subsequently to the Hanoi Medical University.

12. Hoang Dinh Cau, "Report on Consequences of Agent Orange in Vietnam," 10-80 Committee, 2000.

13. Stellman, et al., "extent and patterns," 685.

14. Ministry of Labor, Invalids and Social Affairs, "National Census of Agent Orange Victims in Vietnam," 2005.

15. General Statistics Office of Vietnam, *Vietnam Population and Household Census 2009*. The General Statistics Office conducted the VPHC in April 2009 with technical assistance from the United Nations Population Fund (UNFPA), http://www.gso.gov.vn/default_en.aspx?tabid=515&idmid=5&ItemID=9813. That footnote is mostly in Vietnamese; translation: "For the criteria see Government of Vietnam, Ministry of Health/Ministry of Labor, Invalids and Social Affairs, *Intra-Government Circular on guidelines for determining diseases, disabilities, malformations linked to exposure to toxic chemicals for people who joined the resistance war and their offspring*, Hanoi, November 18, 2013, and Government of Vietnam, Office of the Government, *Decisions — regulations, guidelines for implementing a number of provisions of the Decree in favor of people with meritorious services to the Revolution*, April 9, 2013."

16. For the criteria see Government of Vietnam, Ministry of Health/Ministry of Labor, Invalids and Social Affairs, *Thong Tu Lien Tich Huong Dan Kham Gia Dinh Benh, Tat, Di Dang, Di Tat, Co Lien Quan Den Phoi Nhiem Voi Chat Doc Hoa Hoc Doi Voi Nguoi Hoat Dong Khang Chien, Va Con De Cua Ho*, Hanoi, November 18, 2013; and Government of Vietnam, Office of the Government, *Nghi Dinh-Quy Dinh Chi Tiet, Huong Dan Thi Hanh Mot So Dieu Cua Phap Lenh Uu Dai Nguoi Co Cong Voi Cach Mang*, April 9, 2013.

17. Ibid. The criteria that DAVA applied in 2007 were updated in 2013.

18. The four districts contain two-thirds of Da Nang's population of 887,435 (2009).

19. See chapter 1, Table 1.2.

20. The Vietnam Population and Household Census counts people with disabilities aged five and older. The DAVA data were adjusted to this same age frame.

Chapter 3: Does Dioxin Exposure Lead to Birth Defects and Reproductive Failure?

1. Charles Schmidt, "Is Agent Orange Still Causing Birth Defects?" *Scientific American,* March 16, 2016, http://www.scientificamerican.com/article/is-agent-orange-still-causing-birth-defects/.

2. M. Manikkam, C. Guerrero-Bosagna, R. Tracy, M.M. Haque, M.K. Skinner, "Dioxin (TCDD) Induces Epigenetic Transgenerational Inheritance of Adult Onset Disease and Sperm Epimutations," *PLOS ONE,* September 26, 2012, https://doi.org/10.1371/journal.pone.0046249; M. Manikkam et al., "Transgenerational Actions of Environmental Compounds on Reproductive Disease and Identification of Epigenetic Biomarkers of Ancestral Exposure," *PLOS ONE,* February 28, 2012, https://doi.org/10.1371/journal.pone.0031901.

3. Anh D. Ngo, Richard Taylor, Christine L. Roberts and Tuan V. Nguyen, "Association between Agent Orange and birth defects: systematic review and meta-analysis," *International Journal of Epidemiology* 35, no. 5 (October 1, 2006): 1220–1230, http://ije.oxfordjournals.org/content/35/5/1220.short.

4. Arnold Schecter and John D. Constable, "Commentary: Agent Orange and birth defects in Vietnam," *International Journal of Epidemiology* 35, no. 5 (October 1, 2006): 1230–1232, http://ije.oxfordjournals.org/content/35/5/1230.full.

5. Interview with Le Ke Son and Charles Bailey, Ho Chi Minh City, April 21, 2015.

6. Nguyen Hung Phuc, Thai Hong Quang, Cung Binh Chung and Le Ke Son, "Research on consequences of toxic chemicals sprayed by the U.S. in the south of Vietnam on humans and proposals for activities to overcome them," Ministry of Defense, Hanoi, 1982. Classified document 52.02.05.02; declassified in 2005.

7. Nguyen Van Nguyen, Pham Ngoc Dinh and Le Bach Quang, "Research on long term impacts of Agent Orange on health of humans living near Bien Hoa, Da Nang and Phu Cat Air Bases," Ministry of Defense, Hanoi, 1999. Classified document under Project Z1; declassified in 2002.

8. Le Bach Quang and Doan Huy Hau, "Research on long term impacts of Agent Orange/dioxin on the health of soldiers, veterans and their children and grandchildren and proposed interventions," Committee 33 Research Program, Hanoi, 2005.

9. J. N. Robinson, K. A. Fox, W. G. Jackson, N. S. Ketchum, M. Pavuk, and W. Grubbs, "Air Force Health Study — An Overview," J. Organohalogen Compounds 68 (2006): 752–755.

10. Kido Teruhiko, Tung Van Dao, Manh Dung Ho, Nhu Duc Dang, Ngoc Thien Pham, Rio Okamoto, Muneko Nishijo, Hidewaki Nakagawa, Seijiro Homma, Son Ke Le, Hung Ngoc Nguyen, "High cortisol and cortisone levels are associated with breast milk dioxin concentrations in Vietnamese women, *European Journal of Endocrinology* 170 (2013): 131–139; Kido Teruhiko, Seijiro Homma, Dang Duc Nhu, Ho Dung Manh, Dao Van Tung, Sun Xian Liang, Rie Okamoto, Shoko Maruzeni, Hideaki Nakagawa, Nguyen Ngoc Hung, Le Ke Son, "Inverse association of highly chlorinated dioxin congeners in maternal breast milk with dehydroepiandrosterone levels in three-year-old Vietnamese children," Science of the Total Environment 550 (2016): 248–255.

11. Muneko Nishijo, Pham The Tai, Hideaki Nakagawa, Shoko Maruzeni, Nguyen Thi Nguyet Anh, Hoang Van Luong, Tran Hai Anh, Ryumon Honda, Yuko Morikawa, Teruhiko Kido, Hisao Nishijo, "Impact of Perinatal Dioxin Exposure on Infant Growth: A Cross-Sectional and Longitudinal Studies in Dioxin-Contaminated Areas in Vietnam," *PLOS ONE* 7, no. 7 (July 2012), e40273.

    Pham The Tai, Muneko Nishijo, Tran Nghi Ngoc, Hideaki Nakagawa, Hoang Van Luong, Tran Hai Anh, Hisao Nishijo. "Effects of perinatal dioxin exposure on development of children during the first 3 years of life," Journal of Pediatrics 2016.

    Pham The Tai, Muneko Nishijo, Nguyen Thi Nguyet Anh, Shoko Maruzeni, Hideaki Nakagawa, Hoang Van Luong, Tran Hai Anh, Ryumon Honda, Teruhiko Kido, Hisao Nishijo, "Dioxin exposure in breast milk and infant neurodevelopment in Vietnam," *Journal of Occupational and Environmental Medicine* 70, no. 9 (September 2013): 656–662.

    Tai The Pham, Muneko Nishijo, Anh Thi Nguyet Nguyen, Nghi Ngoc Tran, Luong Van Hoang, Anh Hai Tran, Trung Viet Nguyen, Hisao Nishijo, "Perinatal dioxin exposure and the neurodevelopment of Vietnamese toddlers at 1 year of age," *Science of the Total Environment* 536 (2015): 575–581

    M. Nishijo, T. T. Pham, A. T. N. Nguyen, N. N. Tran, H. Nakagawa, L. V. Hoang, A. H. Tran, Y. Morikawa, M. D. Ho, T. Kido, M. N. Nguyen, H. M. Nguyen and H. Nishijo, "2,3,7,8-Tetrachlorodibenzo-p-dioxin in breast milk increases autistic traits of 3-year-old children in Vietnam," *Molecular Psychology* 19, no. 11 (November 2014): 1220–1226.

12. "Elmo R. Zumwalt 3rd, 42, Is Dead; Father Ordered Agent Orange Use," *New York Times*, August 14, 1988.

13. Interview with James Zumwalt, Rehoboth Beach, Delaware, May 5, 2015.

Chapter 4: Has the Forest Ecology Recovered from the Spraying of Agent Orange?

1. Pamela McElwee, "Agent Orange and Global Environmental Justice: Secondary Effects of Wartime Damage," abstract of paper presented to the American Association of Asian Studies Annual Meeting, Boston, March 22–25, 2007.

2. The team included specialists in vertebrate and invertebrate zoology, botany, medicinal plants, ornithology, herpetology, ichthyology, geography and archeology.

3. Excerpts from the Unpublished Memoirs of Professor Vo Quy, Vietnam National University/Hanoi, Center for Natural Resources & Environmental Studies, Hanoi 2011.

4. Government of Vietnam, Ministry of Natural Resources & Environment and Ministry of Science & Technology, "Harmful effects of Agent Orange/dioxin on humans and the environment," Report of the Summary Research Program-33, 2011–2015, Hanoi, 2016.

5. Vo Quy, "Statement to the House Subcommittee on Asia, the Pacific and Global Environment," June 4, 2009, http://www.internationalrelations.house.gov/111/quy060409.pdf.

6. Vo Quy, "Statement to the House."

7. Wayne Dwernychuk and Charles Bailey, "Facts. The Difference Between Agent Orange and Dioxin," http://www.agentorangerecord.com/information/facts_faqs/facts/.

8. Phung Tuu Boi, "Agent Orange and the Environment: From Research to Remediation," Center for Assistance in Nature Conservation and Community Development, presentation at the American Association of Asian Studies, Boston, March 2007, 35.

9. Boi, "Agent Orange and the Environment," 37.

Chapter 5: What Do Americans Know about Agent Orange, and How Are They Prepared to Help?

1. The Ford Foundation Special Initiative on Agent Orange/Dioxin created and funded the AOVII, a consortium of six American nongovernment organizations with expertise in media outreach: The Communications Consortium Media Center, the Aspen Institute (Washington, D.C.), Active Voice, Asian Americans Pacific Islanders in Philanthropy, San Francisco State University Renaissance Journalism Project and the War Legacies Project (Vermont).

2. Belden Russonello & Stewart (BRS), "Feeling Responsible, Acting Humanitarian: Values that Underlie Support for Addressing Agent Orange in Vietnam — Report of Six Focus Groups on Addressing the Impact of Agent Orange and Dioxin in Vietnam," Washington, October 2009.

3. Ibid., 3.

4. Ibid., 4.

5. Ibid.

6. Ibid., 5.

7. Belden Russonello & Stewart (BRS), "The Case for Addressing the Agent Orange Legacy in Vietnam: Humanitarian Action, Not History, Drives Support — Analysis of a National Survey of Registered Voters," Washington, December 2009.

8. Ibid., 6.

Chapter 6: What is Vietnam Doing for the Victims of Agent Orange?

1. Ordinance No. 04/2012/UBTVQH 13 amending and supplementing Ordinance No. 26/2005/PL-UBTVQH 11 providing the preferential treatment for people with meritorious services to the revolution, amended under Ordinance No. 35/2007/PL-UBTVQH 11.32016-6-27.

2. Office of Committee 33, "Results of Activities to Overcoming the Consequences of Agent Orange/dioxin in Vietnam," Hanoi, 2016

3. Ibid.

4. Ibid.

Chapter 7: What Has the United States Done So Far?

1. Patrick J. Leahy, "Addressing War Legacies in Vietnam," speech at the Center for Strategic and International Studies, Washington, D.C., June 23, 2015, https://dorutodpt4twd.cloudfront.net/content/uploads/files/content/docs/agent-orange/Patrick%20Leahy%20_Addressing%20Agent%20Orange_Speech%20Transcript_CSIS%206.23.2015_0.pdf.

2. Christopher Abrams, USAID/Vietnam email, December 11, 2017.

3. Michael Martin, "U.S. Agent Orange/Dioxin Assistance to Vietnam," Congressional Research Service, November 13, 2015; Mary F. Hayden, Hoang V. Tran, Tra H. Nguyen, Long T. Tran and Chang N.Q. Le, Management Systems International, "Evaluation of Disabilities Programming," USAID/Vietnam, 2015, https://assets.aspeninstitute.org/content/uploads/2016/06/USAID-Disabilities-PE-Report-Final-11182015.pdf.

4. H.R. 2029 Consolidated Appropriations Act, 2016.

5. Charles R. Bailey, "Delivering Services to People with Disabilities Associated with Exposure to Dioxin in Vietnam," Aspen Institute, June 2, 2014, https://assets.aspeninstitute.org/content/uploads/2016/06/2014-6-2_CBailey-Focusing_USG_Delivery_of_Services_for_PWDs_in_Vietnam- EN.pdf.

Chapter 9: Can the Agent Orange Issue Be Resolved through the Courts in the United States or Elsewhere?

1. Dow, Monsanto, Hercules, Northwest Industries, Diamond Shamrock and North American Phillips.

2. Judge Weinstein was born in 1921, served in the United States Navy in World War II and was a law professor at Columbia University. In 1967, President Lyndon B. Johnson appointed Weinstein to the Federal Court, where he continues to serve as of December 2017.

3. Interview with Kenneth Feinberg, June 30, 2015. Feinberg is an American attorney who has specialized in mediation and alternative dispute resolution beginning with the Agent Orange Settlement Fund in 1984. Among his later assignments, he was appointed special master of the U.S. Government's September 11 Victim Compensation Fund. He served as the government-appointed administrator of the BP Deepwater Horizon Disaster Victim Compensation Fund. Feinberg was appointed by the Commonwealth of Massachusetts to administer the victim assistance fund created after the 2013 Boston Marathon bombings.

4. Of the total, $197 million went to American veterans or their survivors, $7 million to Australians and $1 million to New Zealanders.

5. United States Department of Veterans Affairs, Compensation — Agent Orange Settlement Fund, May 14, 2016, http://www.benefits. va.gov/compensation/claims-postservice-agent_orange-settlement-settlementFund.asp.

6. Feinberg interview.

7. Interview with Bobby Muller, May 3, 2015.

8. For details, see U.S. Department of Veterans Affairs, "Benefits Overview for Agent Orange Exposure," http://www.publichealth.va.gov/exposures/agentorange/benefits/index.asp.

9. Phan Thi Phi, Nguyen Van Quy (representing himself and his children Nguyen Quang Trung, Nguyen Thi Thuy Nga), Duong Quynh Hoa (representing herself and her deceased son Huynh Trung Son), Nguyen Thang Loi, Tong Thi Tu, Nguyen Long Van, Nguyen Thi Thoi, Nguyen Minh Chau, Nguyen Thi Nham, Le Thi Vinh, Nguyen Thi Hoa (representing herself and her son Vo Thanh Tuan Anh), Vo Thanh Hai, Nguyen Thi Thu (representing herself and her children Nguyen Son Linh and Nguyen Son Tra), Dang Thi Hong Nhut, Nguyen Dinh Thanh, Nguyen Muoi, Ho Thi Le (representing herself and her deceased husband Ho Xuan Bat), Ho Kan Hai (representing herself and her son Nguyen Van Hoang) and Vu Thi Loan.

10. Dow, Monsanto, Pharmacia, Hercules, Occidental Chemical, Ultramar Diamond Shamrock, Maxus Energy, Thompson Hayward Chemical, Harcros Chemicals, Uniroyal, C.D.U. Holding, Diamond Shamrock, Diamond Alkali, Ansul, Hooker Chemical, Hoffman-Taft Chemicals, Chemical Land Holdings, T-H Agriculture & Nutrition, Thompson Chemical, Riverdale Chemical, Elementis Chemicals, United States Rubber and Syntex.

11. Amended Complaint, United States District Court for the Eastern District of New York, September 13, 2004, paragraphs 246–249, 50–51.

12. Amended Complaint, paragraph 251, 52. Plaintiffs asserted that applicable laws included the Alien Tort Claims Act; Torture Victim Protection Act; War Crimes Act; 1925 Geneva Protocol for the Prohibition of the Use in War of Asphyxiating, Poisonous or Other Gases, and of Bacteriological Methods of Warfare; Article 23 of the Annex to the Hague Convention IV, Respecting the Laws and Customs of War on Land, signed October 18, 1907; Geneva Convention relative to Protection of Civilian Persons in Time of War, signed at Geneva August 12, 1949; Agreement for the Prosecution and Punishment of the Major War Criminals of the European Axis and Charter of the International Military Tribunal at Nuremberg, signed and entered into force August 8, 1945; United Nations Charter, signed at San Francisco on June 26, 1945, and entered into force on October 24, 1945; United Nations General Assembly Resolution No. 2603-A (1969); customary international law; common law of the United States of America; the laws of Vietnam; and common law of the State of New York.

13. The U.S. Supreme Court has ruled that courts should not hear cases that deal with issues the Constitution has made the sole responsibility of the other branches of the federal government, in this case the executive branch's responsibility for the conduct of foreign relations.

14. Statement of Interest of the United States, In re Agent Orange Product Liability Litigation, United States District Court for the Eastern District of New York, February 28, 2005, 1.

15. United States District Court for the Eastern District of New York, In re Agent Orange Product Liability Litigation, Memorandum, Order and Judgment, March 10, 2005, 66.

16. Ibid., 11.

17. Ibid., 17.

18. Ibid., 184.

19. Ibid., 186.

20. Ibid., 24.

21. Ibid., 41–42.

22. Ibid., 18.

23. Vietnam Association for Victims of Agent Orange, et al., Petitioners v. Dow Chemical Company et al., Petition for a Writ of Certiorari in the Supreme Court of the United States, No. 08-470, 6, 22.

24. For background, see Professor Christian Förster, "The Korean Case: Product Liability Approach to Compensation for Damage Caused by Agent Orange," Heidelberg University; paper presented at the conference on "Toxic Legacies: Agent Orange as a Challenge," Rachel Carson Center, Ludwig Maximillian University, Munich; Evangelische Academie Tutzing, June 29, 2015.

25. "Chloracne is a well-established, long-term effect of exposure to TCDD or dioxin, a contaminant in Agent Orange," United States Department of Veterans Affairs, Public Health, "Chloracne," http://www.publichealth. va.gov/exposures/agentorange/conditions/chloracne.asp, accessed December 17, 2017.

26. "South Korea court Orders US Firms to Pay Up over Agent Orange," Fox News World, July 12, 2013, http://www.foxnews.com/ world/2013/07/12/s-korea-court-orders-us-firms-to-pay-up-over-agent-orange.html.

Chapter 10: How Has the Bilateral Relation on Agent Orange Changed Over Time, and What Is the Situation Today?

1. Interview with Bobby Muller, Washington, D.C., May 3, 2015.

2. Muller interview.

3. Richard Goldstein, "Elmo R. Zumwalt Jr., Admiral Who Modernized the Navy, Is Dead at 79," New York Times, January 3, 2000.

4. Interview with James Zumwalt, Rehoboth Beach, Delaware, May 5, 2015.

5. President Bill Clinton, White House press conference, May 28, 1996, http://www.presidency.ucsb.edu/ws/index.php?pid=52876.

6. Interview with Le Van Bang, Ha Tay Province, Vietnam, April 24, 2015.

7. Bang interview.

8. The Thirty Years' War (1618–1648) engaged the major powers of Europe in a struggle between Catholics and Protestants; most of the fighting took place on German soil.

9. Interview with Vu Khoan, Hanoi, April 23, 2015.

10. Khoan interview.

11. Agreement between the Government of the United States of America and the Government of the Socialist Republic of Vietnam Concerning the Settlement of Certain Property Claims, Hanoi, January 28, 1995.

12. Bang interview.

13. Interview with United States Ambassador Ted Osius, Hanoi, January 2015.

14. Lewis M. Stern, "Agent Orange and the Normalization of U.S.-Vietnamese Defense Relations," Institute for National Strategic Studies, National Defense University, Washington, D.C., September 2008, 6.

15. Ford Foundation, Recommendation for Grant Action, Red Cross Society of Vietnam, $150,000, two years from June 1, 2000. See Appendix 3 for a complete list of all Ford Foundation grants related to Agent Orange, 2000–2011.

16. Nguyen Trong Nhan letter to President Bill Clinton, Hanoi, November 18, 2000.

17. Bill Clinton letter to Nguyen Trong Nhan, Washington, D.C., February 12, 2001.

18. Pete Peterson, "U.S. and Vietnam Agree on Agent Orange Study," CNN, July 4, 2001, http://www.cnn.com/2001/WORLD/asiapcf/southeast/07/04/vietnam.agent.orange/.

19. Quoted in Charles Schmidt, "Is Agent Orange Still Causing Birth Defects?" *Scientific American*, March 16, 2016, http://www.scientificamerican.com/article/is-agent-orange-still-causing-birth-defects/.

20. The study was funded by the government of Canada through its overseas assistance arm, the Canadian International Development Agency.

21. L. Wayne Dwernychuk and Hoang Dinh Cau, "Dioxin Reservoirs in Southern Vietnam — A Legacy of Agent Orange," *Chemosphere* 47 (2002): 117–137.

22. Charles Bailey letters to Dr. Tran Manh Hung, director, 10-80 Committee Ford Foundation, Hanoi, May 27, 2002, and July 12, 2002.

23. Ford Foundation, grant to the 10-80 Committee, Ministry of Health, $243,000, two years from September 1, 2002.

24. Stern, "Agent Orange and the Normalization," 6.

25. Charles Bailey meeting with local Vietnamese leaders in the Aluoi Valley, March 20, 2006.

26. Vietnam Association of Victims of Agent Orange statement, March 10, 2006.

27. Le Ke Son, National Steering Committee for Overcoming the Consequences of the Toxic Chemicals Used by the U.S. in the War in Vietnam, March 10, 2006.

28. Conversation with Charles Bailey, Hanoi, Vietnam, April 25, 2006.

29. Nathan Sage first held this position, followed by three Foreign Service officers, Andrew Herrup, Eric Frater and Douglas O'Neill.

30. The Environmental Protection Agency posted Vance Fong to Hanoi for six months as an embassy science fellow. He then continued as technical adviser on remediation until 2013.

31. JAC U.S. co-chairs (all from the Environmental Protection Agency) — Dr. William H. Farland (2006), deputy assistant administrator, Office of Research and Development; Dr. Kevin Teichman (2007–2011), deputy assistant administrator, Office of Research and Development; and Dr. Jennifer Orme-Zavaleta (2012–2014), director, National Exposure Research Laboratory.

JAC Vietnam co-chair — Dr. Le Ke Son, director, Office of the National Steering Committee for the Overcoming of the Consequences of Toxic Chemicals Used by the U.S. in the War in Vietnam (2006–2014).

JAC Members (2006) — Dr. Anne Sassaman, director, Extramural Research and Training, National Institute of Environmental Health and Science; Colonel Mark Chakwin, military attaché, U.S. Embassy; Dr. Marie Haring Sweeney, health attaché, U.S. Embassy; Nathan Sage, environment, science, technology and health officer, U.S. Embassy; Professor Tran Van

Sung, director, Institute of Chemistry, Vietnam Academy of Science and Technology; Pham Van Que, deputy director, Americas Department, Vietnam Ministry of Foreign Affairs; Dr. Pham Quoc Bao, deputy director, Department of Science and Training, Vietnam Ministry of Health; Major General Pham Ngoc Duong, director, Department of Science, Technology and Environment, Ministry of Defense.

32. Minutes, first meeting of Vietnam-U.S. Joint Advisory Committee, Hanoi, June 6, 2006.

33. Interview with Michael W. Marine, Washington, D.C., April 30, 2015.

34. Grants to Vietnam Veterans of America Foundation ($450,000), East Meets West Foundation ($667,800), Institute for Social Development Studies ($170,600) and Vietnam Public Health Association ($175,000) and travel awards to Vietnamese scientists.

35. Jonathan M. Aloisi, deputy chief of mission, U.S. Embassy, letter to Dr. Le Ke Son, January 8, 2007.

36. "In Vietnam, Old Foes Take Aim at War's Toxic Legacy," *Washington Post*, November 13, 2006, 1.

37. Joint Statement Between the Socialist Republic of Vietnam and the United States of America, November 2006, georgewbush-whitehouse.archives. gov/news/releases/2006/11/20061117-4.html.

38. The other initial members were Bui The Giang, director general, People to People Relations Department, Commission for External Relations, Communist Party of Vietnam; Christine Todd Whitman, former governor of New Jersey and president of the Whitman Strategy Group; Professor Vo Quy, Center for Natural Resources and Environmental Studies, Vietnam National University, Hanoi; William E. Mayer, president and CEO, Park Avenue Equity Partners and chairman emeritus, Aspen Institute board of trustees. Membership was expanded from the convener and six members to the convener and ten members and changed over time. Ton Nu Thi Ninh was followed as Vietnamese co-chair by subsequent vice chairs of the Foreign Affairs Committee, Ngo Quang Xuan and Ha Huy Thong. Other new members were Mary Dolan-Hogrefe, vice president and senior adviser, National Organization on Disability, and director, World Committee on Disability; Lieutenant General Phung Khac Dang, vice president, Veterans Association of Vietnam; Dr. Vaughan Turekian, chief international officer, American Academy for the Advancement of Science; Dr. Nguyen Thi Ngoc Phuong, chief of obstetrics gynecology of the Medical University of Ho Chi Minh City and director general of Ngoc Tam Hospital Corporation; and Do Hoang Long, deputy director, People to People Department, External Relations Commission.

39. U.S.-Vietnam Dialogue Group on Agent Orange/Dioxin, "Declaration and Plan of Action 2010-2019," Aspen Institute, Washington, D.C., June 2010.

40. U.S.-Vietnam Dialogue Group on Agent Orange/Dioxin, "First Year Report," June 2011; "Second Year Report," May 2012; and "Third Year Report," September 2013, Aspen Institute, Washington, D.C.

41. Interview with Tim Rieser, May 6, 2015.

42. 110th Congress, U.S. Troop Readiness, Veterans' Care, Katrina Recovery, and Iraq Accountability Appropriations Act, 2007 (P.L. 110-28).

43. Ambassador Michael W. Michalak letter to Senior Lieutenant General Nguyen Huy Hieu, September 28, 2010.

44. Christopher Abrams, USAID/ Hanoi, email, December 3, 2017.

45. Charles R. Bailey, "Delivering Services to People with Disabilities Associated with Exposure to Dioxin in Vietnam," Aspen Institute, June 2, 2014, https://assets.aspeninstitute.org/content/uploads/2016/06/2014-6-2_CBailey-Focusing_USG_Delivery_of_Services_for_PWDs_in_Vietnam- EN.pdf.

46. United States Congress, Appropriations Act, 2016.

47. *Chau, Beyond the Lines* is available on Netflix in the U.S. For background see http://america.cgtn.com/2017/01/03/this-week-on-full-frame-the-power-of-real-life-stories-2.

48. Joint Statement: Between the United States of America and the Socialist Republic of Vietnam, May 23, 2016.

49. Remarks by President Obama in Address to the People of Vietnam, May 24, 2016, https://www.whitehouse.gov/the-press-office/2016/05/24/remarks-president-obama-address-people-vietnam.

50. Joint Statement for Enhancing the Comprehensive Partnership Between the United States of America and the Socialist Republic of Vietnam, the White House, Washington, D.C., May 31, 2017, https://vn.usembassy.gov/20170601-united-states-vietnam-joint-statement-2017/.

51. U.S. Embassy Hanoi, Public Affairs Section, "United States and Vietnam Celebrate Dioxin Remediation at Danang Airport, Commit to Continue Cooperation at Bien Hoa Airbase," Media Release, November 9, 2017, https://vn.usembassy.gov/pr201711010-united-states-vietnam-celebrate-dioxin-remediation-danang-airport-commit-continue-cooperation-bien-hoa-airbase/.

52. The White House, Office of the Press Secretary, "Joint Statement between the United States of America and the Socialist Republic of Vietnam," Washington, November 12, 2017, https://www.whitehouse.gov/the-press-office/2017/11/12/joint-statement-between-united-states-america-and-socialist-republic.

Appendix 1: What Is Dioxin?

1. For further information on the properties of dioxins see http://cfpub.epa.gov/ncea/iris2/chemicalLanding.cfm?substance_nmbr=1024; http://www.dioxinfacts.org/tri_dioxin_data/sitedata/test3/def.html.

2. Exposure to dioxin in the feed induced hepatocellular carcinoma, squamous cell carcinoma of lungs, and hard palate and tongue in Sprague-Dawley rats. Females were more affected by 2,3,7,8-TCDD exposure than males. 2,3,7,8-TCDD was also carcinogenic in mice exposed chronically. See the following references.

   R. J. Kociba, D. G. Keyes, J. E. Beyer, et al., "Results of a two-year chronic toxicity and oncogenicity study of 2,3,7,8-tetrachlorodibenzo-p-dioxin in rats," *Toxicology and Applied Pharmacology* 46 (1978): 279–303.

R. J. Kociba, D. G. Keyes, J. E. Beyer, et al., "Toxicologic studies of 2,3,7,8-tetrachlorodibenzo-p-dioxin (TCDD) in rats," Toxicol Occup Med (De Toxicol Environ Sci) 4 (1978): 281–287.

NTP. 1982b. Carcinogenesis bioassay of 2,3,7,8-tetrachlorodibenzo-p-dioxin (CAS no. 1746-01-6) in Osborne-Mendel rats and B6C3F1 mice (gavage study). Bethesda, Maryland: Carcinogenesis Testing Program, National Cancer Institute, National Institute of Health. Research Triangle Park, North Carolina: National Toxicology Program. (NIH) DHHS publication no 82-1765.

NCI/NTP. 1980. Bioassay of a mixture of 1,2,3,6,7,8-hexachlorodibenzo-p-dioxin and 1,2,3,7,8,9-hexachlorodibenzo-p-dioxin (gavage) for possible carcinogenicity: CAS No. 57653-85-7, CAS No. 19408-74-3. Research Triangle Park, North: U.S. Department of Health and Human Services, Public Health Service, National Institutes of Health/National Toxicology Program. National Cancer Institute Carcinogenesis Technical Report Ser No. 198. NTP no. 80-12.

J. P Carolina, Van Miller, J. J. Lalich, J. R. Allen, "Increased incidence of neoplasms in rats exposed to low levels of 2,3,7,8-tetrachlorodibenzo-p-dioxin," Chemosphere 6 (1977): 537–544.

3. A number of reproductive effects have been observed in animals orally exposed to 2,3,7,8-TCDD, including reduced fertility, pre- and post-implantation losses, decreases in gonad weights, decreased androgen levels, and altered estrus cycle and ovulation. Increased pre- and post-implantation losses were observed in CRCD rats.

E. Giavini, M. Prati, C. Vismara, "Embryotoxic effects of 2,3,7,8-tetrachlorodibenzo-p-dioxin administered to female rats before mating," Environmental Research 31, (1983): 105–110.

G. L. Sparschu Jr., F. L. Dunn Jr., R. W. Lisowe, et al., "Effects of high levels of 2,4,5-trichlorophenoxyacetic acid on fetal development in the rat," Food and Cosmetics Toxicology 9 (1971): 527–530.

F. A. Smith, B. A. Schwetz, K. D. Nitschke, "Teratogenicity of 2,3,7,8-tetrachlorodibenzo-p-dioxin in CF-1 mice," Toxicology and Applied Pharmacology 38 (1976): 517–523.

4. Depletion of lymphocytes results in suppression of T-cell immunity. The T-cell responses studied have included delayed hypersensitivity responses, rejection of skin allografts, and in vitro mutagen responses of lymphoid cells. Effects on T-cells can occur at levels of exposure three orders of magnitude lower than the effects on thymus cellularity.

A. Hanberg, H. Hakansson., U. G. Ahlborg, "ED50" values for TCDD-induced reduction of body weight gain, liver enlargement, and thymic atrophy in Hartley guinea pigs, Sprague-Dawley rats, C57BL/6 mice, and golden Syrian hamsters," Chemosphere 19 (1989): 813–816.

S. D. Holladay, P. Lindstrom, B. L. Blaylock, et al., "Perinatal thymocyte antigen expression and postnatal immune development altered by gestational exposure to tetrachlorodibenzo-p-dioxin (TCDD)," *Teratology* 44, no. 4 (1991): 385–393.

J. Silkworth, D. McMartin, A. DeCaprio, et al., "Acute toxicity in guinea pigs and rabbits of soot from a polychlorinated biphenyl-containing transformer fire." *Toxicology and Applied Pharmacology* 65 (1982): 425–439.

CPSIA information can be obtained
at www.ICGtesting.com
Printed in the USA
LVHW06s0055100818
586498LV00007B/67/P

9 780999 341308